The American Dream

and

What We Must Do to Secure Our Children's Dreams

Dear Ron and Sherrill,

Enjoy the book & God Bless,

Wyatt

Matthew Modleski

First published by Dog Ear Publishing
4010 W. 86th Street, Ste H
Indianapolis, IN 46268
www.dogearpublishing.net

ISBN: 978-145750-366-5

This book is printed on acid-free paper.

Printed in the United States of America

The American Dream

and

What We Must Do to Secure Our Children's Dreams

Flying extremely close formation...upside down...75 feet above the ground at 500 mph tends to generate great interest in the qualities of your formation partner. Mods is a leader, a wingman and a lifelong friend. He is truly a man of integrity, energy and strength. Have you ever known or worked with someone who motivates you to do better, work harder and achieve more? That was my experience with Mods when we served together on the Thunderbird Team and continues to be my experience with Mods to this day. He has a wonderfully inspiring story to share....I know you'll enjoy it as much as I did!

Russ "Puck" Quinn
Thunderbird Solo Pilot
1995-1996

It has been my great privilege to know Matt Modleski since flying with him in Great Britain in the early 90's. Matt is a clear standout among the very select group of young American patriots who have served in our Air Force. His story reflects the unique American characteristic of hard won success through one's own effort, motivated by a laser-like focus on a distant dream. What makes Matt's story even more unique is his particular motivation...Matt is motivated to serve, not to accumulate wealth, fame, or power. It is this sense of dedication to service that brings him to his message in the latter part of his book. He is obviously right. For the sake of my grandchildren and their children, I pray that he can be effective...

Charles D. Link
Major General, USAF (Ret)

It is rare to find a person that is the perfect match for their chosen career, and in the case of the military, rarer still. In 38 years of service I never met or even heard of anyone who could approach the perfection that fit Matt Modleski into the United States Air Force. His story embodies the American Dream. He was born into a hard-working middle-class family in New York State, entered the Air Force after high school and worked his way up the enlisted ranks while pursuing a college degree at night. He was then commissioned, attended flight school and had a remarkable flying career, culminating in his tenure as the Lead Solo of the U.S. Air Force Thunderbird Aerial Demonstration Team. But this story is not the recounting of a military career; rather, it is the tale of a man who stood at a crossroad in his life and chose the more difficult path. The most remarkable thing about Matt, and the most memorable to me, is the ease with which he made the tough choice. That reflects the character of a man who is comfortable with his principles and lives them to their fullest every day. I was lucky to have him work for me; I am blessed to call him friend.

Robert A. Knauff
Major General, USAF (retired)

Every now and then you run into someone in life who seems to standout from their peers not because of what they've accomplished but because of how they accomplish it. When I think of the words integrity, character, honesty and perseverance I think of Matt Modleski. I have known Matt "Mods" Modleski for more than 22 years and it's been a pleasure to watch his service to the nation from up close. I was in attendance when Mods was chosen as the Top Graduate from his Officer Training School class and I was the guest speaker who presented him with his Top Graduate award from his Undergraduate Pilot Training class. The reason I got to know Matt so well is because my son Scott and he were great friends throughout all of that training and because of all his enlisted experience he was a great help to all of his classmates.

Matt and his family have served the nation with honor and distinction. When I endorsed him for his selection to the United States Air Force Thunderbird Team, he was the first man in the more than 20 years since I left the Team to earn my support, and he was a superb Thunderbird Team member after being selected. Enjoy the book and if you have the chance, get to know Matt personally. You'll be glad you did!

Stanton R. Musser
Major General, USAF (Ret)

I am a big believer in strategy...in a nutshell: what it is that one relies upon to achieve their objectives in life. And when I have the opportunity to spend time with individuals, I find myself analyzing them from this same strategic perspective. I think of how I can capture the essence of that person by the way I see them interact with others. I have had the privilege of getting to know Matt not as a US Air Force professional, but first as a client, then a business partner, and also as a friend. I find that he is the same unwavering person in every situation. He is a man of integrity, focus, commitment, loyalty, and faith. Matt's book captures not just the challenges of his chasing every boy's dream of being a fighter pilot, but also what it takes to make not just a name for one's self, but to make a difference in life. I can honestly say Matt fits into that rare category in my life of those to whom I would entrust anything of personal and professional importance.

C. Thomas (Tom) Stovall
President, SGM Inc.

Preface

I'd like to dedicate this book to my entire family: my mom; my dad (we miss him); my brother, Jeff; and my sisters, Lee and Cherie. Thank you all for all the love and support through the years! I also want to thank Dianne and my two boys, Keaton and Jacob. Dianne and I have been married for more than 23 years. Through all the moves, the job changes, the buying and selling of homes, and now the raising of two boys, she's been awesome. For all the years we served the nation together (she was a reserve officer called up in the first Gulf War), I say, "Thank you, honey." Dianne's calling in life is to tend to homebound seniors in the inner city of Indianapolis as a geriatric nurse practitioner. I could not do her job, but her patients love her just as all "us boys" in her home love her. Somehow, she finds the time and energy to love all of us in return, and oh how she loves her patients! Thanks, Di!

It is because I have two boys that I am writing this book, and I hope it accomplishes two things. The first is that I want them to know that in America that you can accomplish anything you'd like to if you set goals and develop the character required to persevere and achieve those goals. Heck, if their old man can fly for the United States Air Force Thunderbirds, the world is their oyster if they'll work hard. The first part of the book should help answer the question "Who is this guy Matt 'Mods' Modleski and how was his perspective shaped?"

The second reason I wrote this book, and the purpose of part two, is to engage America in a dialogue that we must have in terms of the trajectory of our country, why we're on that trajectory, and **what we as Americans can do about it**. I am so proud of our nation, and of the American people who make it the best place in the world to live. The focus of this book's chapters forms the foundation of what makes America the finest nation in the world and gives me great hope in our future. These things are **family, big dreams, competitive spirit, accountability, perseverance, and faith**. I have chosen to write about these areas of my life from my time on the Thunderbirds as well as other times in life that show where these core American values were developed. Part one is not written chronologically; rather, it is written in small anecdotes that support each of the themes of the book. I hope you are inspired by the finest team in the world, the US Air Force Thunderbirds (yes, I'm biased) and also learn a bit about the American Dream that took me there.

Finally, I have to say thank you to Michele Dubroy. We met briefly in 1998 during my last week on the Thunderbirds. She called me from out of the blue in October 2009 to begin working on a bigger project for which she has done many interviews with many of the people I've loved throughout my life. It is from her interviews that I have included quotes from some of those I mention in the book. Thank you, Michele!

The center of every man's existence is a dream.

G. K. Chesterton

In dreams begin responsibilities.

William Butler Yeats

Foreword

I t is not uncommon for a young boy or girl to dream of flying. After watching an elite flying team like the Air Force Thunderbirds or the Navy's Blue Angels, it is not unusual for a child to visualize becoming one of these intrepid aviators; thrilling crowds and defying death. But there are two things that make Matt Modleski's journey to achieve his dream of flying for the Thunderbirds special. Firstly, the fact that he was able to obtain his dream despite seemingly insurmountable obstacles; following a path not often taken and littered with naysayers. And secondly, his dream itself was different.

If we're inclined to dream along these lines, most of our dreams end on the flight line greeting the crowds, or in the cockpit executing a knife edge pass. For me, and perhaps for others like me, the dream of flying grew from a sense of adventure and excitement. My dream took root even before the seeds of patriotism were sown. Matt's dream, however, always seemed bigger. From the beginning, his dream to fly was part of larger vision that included service to country and service to others.

As you might expect, this short book will chronicle Matt's journey to become a Thunderbird pilot. It will give you insight into who Matt is, the values that made it possible for him to overcome setbacks, and the family and friends that helped him along the way. But it will also include the acknowledgement that, as Yates stated, "In dreams begin responsibilities."

If your dream is built on service to others and service to our nation, then one of the responsibilities implied is the requirement to identify ways we've gone astray and ways we can be better. This is a necessity, even when those being served are reluctant to accept the observation. Or as Max Depree explained in his book, *The Art of Leadership*, "The first responsibility of a leader is to define reality." This is true even if the reality is at times unpleasant.

In our case, the reality is that we are a great nation, built on solid values, made up of wholesome, hard-working people from diverse backgrounds. But another part of that reality is that in some ways, many of which Matt will identify in this book, we have lost focus and direction. Our nation stands at a crossroads, and although this national self-examination may be painful, we cannot hope to select the correct way forward without going through this process.

Lance Schroeder, Lt. Colonel, USAF Retired

The pessimist sees difficulty in every opportunity.
The optimist sees the opportunity in every difficulty.

Winston Churchill, British prime minister

Introduction

by Lance Schroeder

I n May of 1989, I arrived at RAF Bentwaters, England, for my first operational Air Force tour. I was assigned to fly the A-10 Thunderbolt II, affectionately known as the Warthog, for the 78th Tactical Fighter Squadron. With a lovely home on the stunning western shoreline of the North Sea, and my beautiful wife Jean by my side, I was living my dream.

A standard overseas tour in the Air Force is about three years. As a squadron loses experienced pilots, recent graduates of the Air Force's undergraduate pilot training (UPT) replenish the ranks. The 78th had undergone a substantial turnover just prior to my arrival, so I was I joined in the squadron by several new lieutenants. I'd known many of these fine men as classmates at the Air Force Academy. Together, we'd gone from basic cadets to Air Force officers, fledgling aviators to newly minted fighter pilots. Now we committed ourselves to the task of learning our new job.

The 78th had an exceptional cadre of flight leaders, instructors, and evaluators that led us along the way. But flight instruction, debriefings, and guided study are only part of the process of generating a fully mission-ready fighter pilot. To truly become assets for the squadron, new pilots must take the initiative. They need to put in long hours of mission study, film review, and threat analysis, so along with the other new lieutenants, I spent hours preparing to become a combat-ready asset to our squadron.

Having spent four years of often painstaking training at the academy and an extremely intense year of UPT, we were finely attuned to the dedication and self-motivation being asked of us. And for the most part, we thrived in this atmosphere.

By the time the next wave of lieutenants arrived a couple of months later, we were already well on our way to becoming fully qualified A-10 wingmen. Among the new arrivals was a young Lieutenant Matt "Mods" Modleski. As I'm certain is often the case, the new guys, by virtue of their relative inexperience, were, for the most part, ignored by those of us further along in training. We eagerly delegated the tasks, such as stocking the snack bar and feeding the squadron mascot (an Indian python named Barney), to our juniors. But beyond that, we relied on our contemporaries and our instructors as we continued our preparations. It didn't take long, however, for us to realize that there was something different, something special, about the way the *new guy*, Mods, approached the job.

Most of our study took place in *the safe*. It was literally a safe, enclosed by hardened walls, secured by a thick metal door, with access controlled by a large dial combination lock. The security was required because much of the material regarding our weapon systems, and the systems of our potential enemies, was classified. We spent hours in the safe, poring over documents. I don't think I ever once entered the safe without seeing Mods already camped out, engrossed in a manual. Nor do I recall ever leaving the safe without Matt still sitting at a desk, cup of coffee in hand, reviewing the next article.

Through the next phases of training, when our study increasingly became reviewing film passes of our own practice bombing and gunnery runs, Mods was there, remote (and coffee) in hand. While most of our film review was limited to our instructor's and, subsequently, our individual assessments, Mods took it to the next level. In the hall outside the briefing rooms, he flagged down other flight leaders and asked for their evaluations; he reviewed film of the squadron's top weapons-delivery aces to glean lessons learned; he even asked for our opinions.

I thought that I had been dedicated and determined, but watching Matt's energy, enthusiasm, and motivation made me redouble my efforts. It wasn't long before Matt's labors bore fruit. Even as a *new guy*, Mods began winning gunnery competitions. Not long after that, our squadron (one of four in the wing) began consistently winning the wing level, highly prized, gunnery competitions.

Albert Einstein once said, "Setting an example is not the main means of influencing another; it is the only means." Certainly, the squadron's leadership was responsible for a large part of our success, but for my money, the success of those of us new to the squadron, which contributed greatly to the success of the squadron as a whole, could be traced to Matt's influence.

At the academy, I had the opportunity to read a lot about leadership. In my time in the Air Force, I'd seen a lot of good and, occasionally, bad leaders. I had learned from both types. But here was something new to me. It was obvious that even though Matt was still a very young lieutenant, he was already an exceptional leader, influencing outcomes well beyond his rank. How had that happened?

Matt's work ethic was inspiring. But there was more to it. I studied the way Mods interacted with others. He treated everyone with respect. He cared about the troubles of the airmen in the Life Support shop. He listened to and encouraged the dreams of young administrative clerks. And people responded.

It wasn't long before Matt and I became great friends. Together, we became flight leads, instructors, and eventually evaluators. In that final role, we worked together along with some additional dear friends, including Brigadier General Select Pat Malackowski, on a staff, setting and evaluating standards for the wing. Although our work on that "team" took place over 20 years ago, it remains my finest professional memory.

To understand how Matt was able to inspire and lead so effectively at such a young age, you need to know a little bit about his background. Mods had the audacity to dream big. From his boyhood home in rural America, he dreamed of one day representing his country as an Air Force fighter pilot. His journey was not a typical one. It began with him enlisting in the Air Force at the age of 17 and promptly being told he would never fly. He became a jet engine mechanic and met a man named Roger Henry, who further inspired Matt to reach for his Thunderbird dream. His journey continued.

In the Air Force, you must be an officer in order to become a pilot. So Matt applied for a Reserve Officer Training Corp (ROTC) scholarship. The pilot training portion of his application was declined on the basis of his vision. Mods applied for, and was accepted to, air traffic controller (ATC) school. A flight physical is a recurring requirement for controllers, and it was during one of these physicals that Matt's journey took a turn. The physician indicated that Matt's vision was satisfactory for Air Force pilot qualification!

Mods was selected to attend officer training school (OTS) and UPT after his first application was denied. Again, Matt excelled after a rough start in OTS and was off to pursue his dream and attend UPT. After graduating at the top of his UPT class, Mods received an assignment to fly A-10s at RAF Bentwaters. At this point, our paths first crossed.

This brief chronology does not do justice to the perseverance and competitive spirit required for Matt to get to this point. But it does explain, in part, why Matt arrived at Bentwaters so much more mature and ready to lead than I had been at that point. And, hopefully, it will set the stage for you as we join Matt's narrative. As you read along, take note of Matt's reliance on family, friends, and faith. Throughout it all, I'm certain you'll detect, woven between events and circumstance, Matt's overriding dreams, passions, and desire to serve.

Enjoy!

Perseverance is not a long race;
it is many short races one after another.

Walter Elliott

PART ONE

America's Team!

"Standby hack, let's hack now." Russ Quinn had just given me my 32-second warning, and I counted to myself, one, two, and then I pressed my stopwatch and watched the second hand begin to sweep. I pushed the throttle on my beautiful red, white, and blue F-16 forward slightly and lowered the nose gently while pulling her into a slow left arc. I had done this hundreds of times in practice, and now it was showtime. "Ninety to the line," came Russ's next command. I breathed deeply on my oxygen mask and checked my stopwatch and my orientation to the show line. I was exactly 10 seconds into the maneuver and precisely 90 degrees to the line (meaning my jet was perpendicular to the show line just as we had practiced). That gave me 20 seconds to get to my next checkpoint. I pushed the throttle forward a bit further, felt the acceleration, and continued to pull my fighter through her left turn; now the adrenaline began to pulse. My breathing quickened ever so slightly as I searched for my references on the ground, watched my airspeed build, and waited for Russ's next call. I was now at 125 feet above the ground, 425 knots, accelerating. "Knife-edge," came the radio call from Russ.

"Knife-edge," I yelled into my oxygen mask, indicating that I was on time and exactly two miles away from show center. I pushed the throttle to full military power, accelerated to 475 knots, and looked for Russ.

"Eight thousand…smoke," came Russ's call. I flicked the smoke switch on with my left thumb.

"Six Tally," I said, indicating that I saw Russ and was now responsible for ensuring at more than 1000 miles per hour of closure rate that I would miss him.

Russ called, "Six thousand," and my check point lined up. I pulled the power back to maintain 475 knots, stacked slightly high to obtain the perfect optical picture for the crowd. Russ called, "Ready, hit it," and I banked my fighter left with full stick force toward his in a 90-degree bank while simultaneously stepping on the right rudder. "Roll out," came the call, and I with equal force rolled back right to wings level while simultaneously shutting off my smoke and beginning a smooth pull to 22.5 degrees nose high. I pushed gently to stop the climb, executed a 270-degree roll to the right, and pulled to clear the show line.

"Five's clear, six's clear." We had just completed the opposing knife edge pass; I was living my dream!

Family

I was born in rural America, in a small farming community nestled between the beautiful Catskill Mountains and the Berkshire Hills, East Chatham, New York. Our town had no more than 500 people and no stoplights. We were by all definitions a "hick town" in today's vernacular. I absolutely loved it. My best friend was my cousin Joe. We were together almost every moment of every day growing up, including planned days off from school with sore throats that miraculously cleared up during the morning so we could play in the afternoon.

Small-town America today still holds dear many of the elements that our country was founded on. Family and faith are still more important than the size of one's home or the type of car one drives. Everyone is willing to help a neighbor, because every neighbor is essentially a family member.

My mom and dad loved us. My mom worked tirelessly around the house, keeping all four of us kids clean and fed and feeling secure in our family. I remember my mom's seemingly endless routine of washing and hanging clothes outside, fixing meals, doing dishes, and helping four children do all we needed to do to get ready for school. She did almost all of those tasks alone, as was the "standard" for stay-at-home moms in the '60s.

My father was a strict man who lost his own mother when he was twelve. He was not overtly affectionate with us, but he displayed his affection for me through observing my participation in sports and always being there for those events. When I was a sophomore, our JV baseball team played for the division title at 3 PM on a work day in

Jamestown, New York, some 60 miles from home. There were only one or two dads in the stands as we won that title, and Paul Modleski, my dad, was one of them.

My father almost always worked two jobs to provide for our family. We enjoyed the benefits of his hard work, but he was out of the house often. As a result, time with my father was precious and one of my favorite activities was to get him to take me up to the school to hit fly balls to me. I would have stayed out for many hours playing, but we usually lasted less than an hour. If my dad got thirsty, he would blast one over the fence and then grab his beer while I went to retrieve the ball. Sometimes my throws in to him were wild, resulting in long searches through the leaves in the adjoining woods. He'd say when he found the ball that it was from all the expertise he had developed looking for his golf balls in the woods.... My dad did have a sense of humor.

My dad tended to drink too much beer, and ultimately, he would declare himself an alcoholic. I think every person in the world has their demons, and my father certainly had his. Like all families, we struggled with those demons at times, but in the end, our family persevered. Through my father's own toughness and discipline, he climbed that mountain, conquered that demon, became sober, and never touched alcohol again; my dad was a tough man, and his toughness and perseverance were examples that we all learned from. My mother was a saint!

My mom lost her dad when she was two or three, and the only man she knew as her dad was her step-dad, John Bemiss. "Gramp" loved us kids, and he was a wonderful man. He fed his family during the Great Depression through outdoor skills like hunting, fishing, and trapping.

He shared all of those skills with us as we grew up learning from him. He was a most patient man (most of the time), and the greatest gift Gramp Bemiss passed along to me was showing me how to be happy with very little in life. He loved being outdoors, and material wealth mattered little to him. He may still be the greatest gift God gave me in terms of seeing what real balance in life looks like.

As I said, I played outside continuously with my cousin Joe and our other friends. I remember fishing all day while eating cow corn from the farmer's field; pulling up a potato or beet for lunch was not at all atypical, either. I knew to be home for dinner; that was my only boundary most days.

Moving to Western New York

When I learned we were moving to West Seneca, a suburb of Buffalo, New York, I was nervous, sad, and excited. I was nervous because I was a country kid who had never travelled anywhere outside a 150-mile circle from home. I was excited because it seemed like it was a very large adventure that would take me "all the way to Buffalo," and that sounded very cool. I was sad, of course, to leave my friends, especially my cousin Joe, who was like my brother.

We moved the summer before my 7th grade year, leaving my brother, Jeff, behind with Gramp Bemiss for his senior year at Chatham High School. My brother had a blast with his somewhat less structured environment, but my older sister, Lee, was not happy with the move. As a sophomore, she went from a class of 40 to a class of 500. It was a huge move at her station in life, and I felt bad for her. My younger sister, Cherie, and I seemed to make the move relatively easily, and I remember being very excited about all of the new sports opportunities a large town offered.

I played organized football for the first time in 8th grade, and I really liked it. I also learned quickly that while I had been a standout athlete in my little hometown of East Chatham, New York, I was a slightly above average (average is the key word) athlete in a big-city suburb. I loved sports, was hypercompetitive, and really had a very normal junior high and high school experience. I didn't have to study hard to get decent grades; that was good, because girls and cars had found their way into my life and both of them were taking up a good deal of time.

Dianne—My Better Half

Dianne and I have been married for 23 years, and we have had what I would call a fantastic marriage (I think she would say the same). The spouses of military members sign up for a life and a "bucket of stuff" that most Americans simply won't tolerate: constant moving, long-term deployments away from home to very dangerous parts of the world, and the lack of stability in schools or a home to name a few. Additional items "in the bucket" are the inability to visit families in times of need, and the subordination of the spouse's career for the family to fully serve the nation. It is a very large bucket of stuff, indeed, and Dianne was a gift from God to join me on the journey we have taken together over these many years. I'd love to tell you that we have never had a cross day with one another…yeah, right. I can unequivocally tell you that almost all of our days together have been days that we've been true partners on the journey. Dianne knew from the beginning the commitment that would be required to pursue my dreams in the Air Force, and she signed on with enthusiasm and love. It helped that she served as a military officer and nurse both on active duty and in the reserves from 1985 to 1998.

As a parent, Dianne has been our catalyst for a family more strongly anchored in our faith. She attended a Christ Renews His Parish retreat in 2006 and immediately suggested I do the same. To this day, it remains one of the best steps in strengthening our faith and our family that we have taken together. The retreat forced both of us to detach from the "noise" of daily American life, to pray with more focus, and to listen for answers to those prayers with more patience. It helped us to begin living with more accountability toward our faith, and it was an awesome experience.

Dianne is a great mom, a wonderful wife, and a passionate provider of care to the homebound seniors she cares for in her vocation. She is also the soul mate God brought to me on that fateful day when we first met at Delaware Airpark more than 25 years ago.

Proposal

Dianne and I went to the Poconos on a ski trip in the winter of 1986, a little more than a year since we had first dated in the fall of 1985. I had decided to ask Dianne to marry me, and so while she was at work one day, I took a ring from her house and went to the jewelers to see what a staff sergeant could afford in terms of engagement rings. It turned out that I could actually buy a ring that I was proud to give to Di and so I was ready for the big day.

After our first day of skiing, we went back to the hotel to get cleaned up before heading out for dinner. It was the moment. I was a bit nervous and anxious, but I got down on a knee and brought the ring out and said, "Di, will you marry me?"

She looked a bit surprised and, no kidding, said, "You really want to marry ME?"

In a slightly agitated tone, I said, "You're supposed to say yes or no," to which she said yes, gave me a big hug and kiss, and then said she was going to take me out for a lobster dinner. She called her mom to share the news, and the lobster was good! The rest is, as they say, history.

From One Family to the Next

My family was always the centerpiece of my life. We were not in any way a perfect family then, nor are we today. I learned along the way that no family is perfect, despite what it may look like from the outside. Yet this type of family tie has bound our nation together since its inception. Small-town America still understands and benefits from the view of family that I was fortunate enough to grow up with and experience. It would be my next family, my Air Force family that would supplement and complement the small-town values that came with me when I joined.

The Thunderbird Family

Every fighter squadron in the Air Force is a closely knit unit; I've never been in one that was closer than the Thunderbirds. That fact would be played out for me over and over again right up until the day I left the squadron. I'd only been there a few weeks when the roller-coaster ride of the assignment would be put in humbling perspective and my Thunderbird family would go into help mode.

The Air Force is a family in and of itself; the Thunderbirds are yet another family within that Air Force family. On the Thunderbirds, each year's team has to gel and mold together through the training season, as half of the demo pilots are new each year. That process takes turns and twists along the way. For example, it is always a hard adjustment for the second-year demo pilots to learn to fly off of a new boss. Their only experience has been flying off of a second-year boss up until that transition. The foundation for the team during this transition between show seasons really comes from the attitude, leadership, and example set by the boss, Thunderbird One.

Just as the team must grow and bond for the good of the mission, the new spouses must integrate themselves into the existing support structure, and they too gel and take on their own personality as a group. Much like the leadership impact that the boss has on the team overall, his wife has a similar impact on the attitude and growth of the families on the team.

We were very fortunate to have Heidi Mumm as the lady responsible for setting the tone and tenor for our family within a family. Heidi was easygoing and a true bonding force for the families. She was also energetic and always upbeat, which is a real asset as the time on the road takes its toll on the families left behind. Dianne and Heidi hit it off from the beginning.

Carey Seely was already a great friend of ours from our A-10 days in the same Squadron in England. Her husband, Tony, and I flew A-10s together there, and he was flying the right wing, #3 position, in his second season on the team in 1996. Carey and Dianne were like two sisters who had been reunited after a few years apart, and their conversations picked up where they had left off several years earlier.

Scott Cerilli made the team at the same time I did, and he would fly the left wing, #2 position, in 1996 and 1997. His wife, Kari, was also new to the wives group, and she and Dianne also became fast friends. It didn't take any time at all before the group of wives and families formed strong friendships, alliances, and joint commitments to help one another with children, pets, family emergencies, and everything else.

Little did we know as we embarked on this journey in late 1995 just how much we would come to lean on each and every member of our team for support through the ups and downs that would come over the next two and a half years.

Friends and Enduring Friendships

My life has been blessed by many friends, and I still have some very close friends from all times in life. Doctor Thomas "Champ" Summers and I played football in high school and remain very close to this day. His advice and counsel as a world-class radiologist would prove to be a godsend during my years on the team. My best friend from my youth, Joe Young, who also happens to be my cousin, and I are friends who don't see one another nearly enough, but when we do, it's like old times. These enduring friendships are really the jewels in our lives. While none of the friends mentioned in this book (except Joe) are truly family, they are all part of what I consider to be family: my Air Force family and my Thunderbird family.

Most of my dear friends are my military friends. We have shared a common bond that is similar to one that might result from the combination of being family member and best friend all at once. When the cause of friendship is shared sacrifice and service to the nation, the bond that develops is hard to articulate. Rather than run the risk of talking about all of my military friends and leaving someone out, I'm going to talk about a few of my closest friends and groups of friends and let you get to know them like I do.

The Jet Engine Years

In July 2007 one of my friends from our jet engine days e-mailed to say he thought it might be a good idea for us to get together to celebrate the life of the oldest member of our group by surprising him for a reunion. So, with a bit of planning, many of us got on planes from around the country and flew into Lubbock, Texas, to meet and surprise RM Salmon, our friend. The reunion was a blast, and while more than 20 years had all of us looking older, it was like no time had passed at all as we sat and laughed about our days together serving the nation and our Air Force. To this day, we can dial one another up on the phone and, though many years may have passed between conversations, it's as if we just spoke the day before; the camaraderie that was once there has never gone away. In June 2010, three years after our reunion, our friend RM passed away, leaving us all saddened. His wife Marlene has great faith in God, and her strength has been an inspiration to all of us as we have said good-bye to a very dear friend.

My Controller Buddies

The next group of friends came from my days as an air traffic controller. What I remember most from those days is that we worked hard and we played hard as a group. Our days off together as a crew didn't coincide with more normal jobs that had no shift work. In other words, our days off constantly rotated so, more often than not, our days off did not align with the weekend. What that resulted in was a group of people who worked hard and then shared a lot of off-duty time together as well. Whether playing sports, going to the beach, or going out on the town, we had a blast and created lifelong friendships that remain today. In the summer of 2009, I flew into Dover, Delaware, after working with a client on the East Coast, and I had a mini-reunion with three friends from my days as a controller. Once again, it was as if the years apart had never existed, and after many crabs (a Dover specialty) and too many beers, we parted ways for what I'm sure will be several more years.

Pilot Training and Beyond

Scott Musser, Greg Imrich, and I were friends in pilot training after graduating from officer training school together. Greg and I lived in the same apartment complex, and Scott's wife, Janeal, and my wife, Dianne, were both nurses and found jobs together at the same hospital after we relocated to the Phoenix area. Greg's wife, Diane, also worked, and the six of us bonded almost immediately and became lifelong friends.

Undergraduate pilot training is very time intensive academically and it is both mentally and physically draining. If one hopes to do well, cooperation in studying and learning is mandatory. Scott, Greg, and I were a team. Think of it as a combination of studying for the biggest academic final of your high school or college life combined with playing in the biggest sporting event of your life as well; now think about doing it every week for a year. That describes pilot training. Scott and Greg were the guys who helped me most to succeed in that environment, and I hope in some small way, I helped them as well. We studied together and hung out on the weekends together (studying and playing), and our wives were as close as we were. We will forever share experiences and friendships forged in that environment, because they are friendships and trust that last a lifetime.

After pilot training came A-10 training and then an assignment to RAF Bentwaters/Woodbridge in England. Again, there are too many people from those days for me to mention all of them, but I feel compelled to mention three men who represent all that is great about those who serve our nation wearing the uniform.

Lance Schroeder and I met as lieutenants in the 78th Tactical Fighter Squadron. He was an academy graduate who was quiet, smart, and hardworking. He also looked like he was 17 years old; I couldn't believe it. Then I met his beautiful wife, Jean; she looked to be several years his junior, and I wondered what kind of water they were drinking. I wanted some of it. I had more meaningful conversations about the nation, the Air Force, leadership, fighter pilot stuff, and other related topics with Lance than with almost anyone else I have ever known. What I respected most about Lance is that he was always willing to look at a problem from an alternative perspective. In short, his quiet demeanor masked a brilliant mind that the nation and the Air Force benefitted greatly from every day.

Another officer who worked with Lance and me and shared in some of these deep conversations was Pat Malackowski. Pat, Lance, and I all worked together for a period of about a year in Standards and Evaluations. Aside from my assignment as a Thunderbird pilot, this was the best year of my Air Force life in terms of job satisfaction. Pat is a true American, a high-quality leader and a warrior through and through. He is still serving on active duty in the Air Force and was selected to the rank of brigadier general in February 2011. We are lucky to have him there standing guard. Well done, Pat!

Lance and I went on to serve together again in Tucson as instructor pilots, and Dianne and I were asked to be godparents for Luke, one of Lance and Jean's five children (Ryan, Luke, Rose, Grace, and Annie). We accepted, honored to be asked. My final comments about Lance and Jean are these: They have always been model parents for Dianne and me. We will never come close to their skills in this arena. Their compassion and patience with their children makes ours pale in comparison, and when life winds down for all of us and we're relaxing and reflecting on the blessings we've shared together, I can tell you what I will say about Lance and Jean. I will be able to point to their children and honestly say they were the most important thing in Lance and Jean's lives and that Lance and Jean behaved that way every single day with their actions. They are a great example for all of us who parent, and I'm incredibly thankful for having been blessed to know them.

Tony Seely was a captain and a bit senior to Lance and me when I arrived at the 78th Tactical Fighter Squadron; he was a guy you simply could not help liking. Tony wrestled in high school and was the captain of the wrestling team at the Air Force Academy; he was also a very good fighter pilot. He was, in the mold of Lance, quiet most of the time, with a wild streak that surfaced occasionally, usually during low-altitude flight. (As it turned out, Tony's eye for 250 feet above the ground was better than most of ours; we just thought he was low. We found out he was really at 250 once radar altimeters were installed in our jets.) As I mentioned earlier, his wife's name is Carey, and they lived around the corner from us in a small British neighborhood. How I loved to make Tony and Carey laugh, and laugh they did; we had a blast. Dianne and Carey became great friends, and we vacationed together, worked hard together, and came to have great respect for one another. When the Seelys left England, it was a sad day for us, but it would turn out that our lives would again be reconnected as Thunderbird teammates. To put it in literal terms, we were never closer professionally as I flew off Tony's wing some 3 feet away during all of our 6-Ship Delta formation flying. Our time on the Thunderbirds together simply further cemented our friendship, as well as that of Dianne and Carey.

Tony and Carey have been nothing short of inspirational as parents to their three children, Matthew, Hadleigh, and Hannah. Tony still serves the nation on active duty after returning to service following the 9-11 attacks. Whenever I have the chance to spend time with the Seelys, I do, as their commitment to their faith and their family is a shining example for all of us. I will cherish their friendship forever.

The final two friends I'll talk about in this book are Russ Quinn and Mark Arlinghaus, or, as I know them, Puck and Lefty. They were the two men I flew with on the Thunderbirds who occupied the "other" solo pilot slot during my two-year tour. Russ was my lead solo during the 1996 season, and Lefty was my opposing solo during the 1997 season. You learn a great deal about someone's character, drive, determination, and attention to detail when you're hurtling toward one another with 1200 miles per hour of closure and it's the other guy's job to miss you. And so we learned about each other and came to have as much respect for one another as is humanly possible.

Puck, as it turned out, did not want me as his opposing solo. It wasn't personal; it was simply that Russ had flown F-16s his whole career, and when Scott Cerilli and I were selected to the team at the end of 1995 for the 1996 season, Scott had flown F-16s and I had flown A-10s. Russ didn't want a "Hog pilot," as his solo brother (a term we would use together on the team and still do), but the funniest thing of all is that I didn't know any of that until we had completed our training season and it slipped out one day during a discussion with most of the 12 officers present. By then, our bond had been established and it was nothing more than fodder for jokes, as it remains to this day.

Puck and I came up through the Air Force in very different ways. He went to a prep school and then was accepted into the academy, where he played Division I hockey (hence the call sign Puck), and he went from there to pilot training and straight to the F-16, where he excelled. He went to Fighter Weapons School, where he again applied 100% effort and graduated from one of the toughest courses that fighter pilots attend. He was and is, by every definition of the word, a professional fighter pilot. My journey through the enlisted ranks, officer school, pilot training, and then the A-10 was unique in its own way, but weapons school graduates sometimes have an edge that makes most conversations with them one-way. It was one of those one-way conversations with Puck that I abruptly halted one day which set our friendship on a new path and took our professional relationship to a new level. Here's the story in Puck's words:

> *During the training season, I was going through some significant stress at home. I had already been through one training season and one show season. My wife at the time was pretty much fed up with the road time away and the long hours while I was home. That strain was starting to show at work, and I was not the friendliest guy around. To make matters worse, the solos always had the first takeoff during training season...right at sunrise. That meant getting up for an 0520 brief and an 0650 takeoff. One morning, Mods and I got into a bit of an argument in the debrief about something....I don't even remember what it was...and I said something to the effect of "hey Jack...xxxxxxx." Mods shot right back at me and explained two things to me very clearly: number one, that I had better get my shit together if I was going to fly with him, and number two, that he really was on my side and recognized the stress I was under. I realized after that exchange that this was a very extra-ordinary man.*

Puck took seriously every aspect of being a Thunder-bird. He was kind to all of the people we met on the road. He flew with precision, focus, and a desire to be better each day that was unsurpassed on the team, and most of all, he did it while struggling personally in his marriage at the time. I remember thinking as Russ worked through those challenges how hard it must be to stay focused on a very precise job while dealing with the distractions that come when a marriage struggles. I think his example helped me a great deal when I would face similar personal challenges with my dad's failing health in 1997 and the need to remain absolutely focused while strapped into the cockpit.

Russ is remarried to a beautiful woman named Margie, and they have a wonderful son named Ryan. Russ remains to this day one of my very best friends in the world. When he retired from the active duty Air Force in 2011, we were worse off as an Air Force as a result. Out of our friendship on the team has grown a friendship that will last a lifetime between an F-16 professional and his "Hog buddy." He is my solo brother, but in every other way, he is like my real brother, Jeff, who means the world to me in a way that only brothers can.

Lefty Arlinghaus came to the team in 1997 and, to be honest, watching Russ Quinn walk away from the team after establishing such a deep friendship, it was a bit awkward "starting over" with Lefty. Anyone who has ever met Lefty would come away with two thoughts: "He's a hell of a nice guy" and "Man, is he smart." His easygoing style hid his genius intellect for a while, but when one of his family members let slip very late in 1997 that he had graduated #1 in his high school class of 800, I wasn't surprised at all. His father is a leading researcher at MD Anderson in Houston, and brains are in the DNA of the Arlinghaus family.

Lefty and I hit it off relatively quickly for one reason: his professionalism! Everything Lefty does, he does with perfection as the objective. That may sound weird—or maybe it sounds normal if you think of a Thunderbird demonstration in terms of the objective—but I'm not talking about just flying. I'm not even talking about just his job. I'm talking about EVERYTHING Lefty does. He does everything with the objective of perfection, and with extreme professionalism. He also has a wild streak that lies very deep at his core, and every now and then, when that streak is let loose, Lefty is the life of the party. It was let loose a few times in the air, and it scared us all. Many days, Lefty and I would spend time talking about leadership, the nation, the Air Force, and our families. I loved those conversations because Lefty's intellect left no stone unturned in the conversation and he challenged every assumption or assertion with questions of his own. It probably comes as no surprise that Lefty and Lance Schroeder were friends at the academy and remain friends to this day. Mark's commitment to being a good officer was at least as important to him as his commitment to being a good pilot, and I respected him immensely for it. The only commitment that's greater to Lefty than his professional commitment is his commitment to his faith and his family.

Lefty over-married (like many of us) to a beautiful woman named Tania. They have two lovely girls named Bailey and Riley, and at the center of their family is their faith in God and Jesus Christ. They have been an inspiration for Dianne and I as parents and as stewards of our own faith in our family. Tania is as bright as Lefty, and the two of them are as dynamic a couple as you will ever meet. They keep their priorities straight and live their life according to those priorities every single day. My only regret is that we don't see the Arlinghauses as much as we'd like to, as they live in Houston and we live in Indiana. But we do get together, and when we do, we discuss the nation, the Air Force, the world, our faith, and our families. Of course we also reminisce about our days together flying red, white, and blue jets around the world as ambassadors for the US and our Air Force. They were great days together with one of the finest men I know in the world.

Here's the thing I take away from all of these friendships that formed as a result of service to the nation in a cause greater than oneself: These are the people I would trust at any time and at any place for the rest of my life. We are friends in a way that I will always cherish and respect, and I don't think I can say it any clearer than that.

Family, Faith, and Friends When I Needed Them Most

I had been in my first training season for about a month and was speaking to my mom on the phone when she broke some news. She told me that my father had been working in the basement, sanding the concrete walls to prepare them for painting and that he had developed a cough. The cough was bad enough that it had produced some blood, and that was concerning enough to schedule a trip to the doctor for a checkup. Mom told me that they would keep me in the loop after the doctor's visit. As promised, Mom did just that, and a few days later, after seeing the doctor, they had some startling news. My father had a large mass in one of his lungs, and he was scheduled for a biopsy of the mass. I remember being shocked at the news and yet hopeful that the news from the biopsy would be better than we expected. It was not, and a few days later, I sat in Las Vegas, Nevada, stunned to hear that my dad had lung cancer. My Thunderbird family rallied around me for the first of many ups and downs during my two-and-a-half-year tour, and Dianne and I hopped on a plane to go home to Buffalo, New York, to be with my dad for his lung surgery. Being allowed to travel home to be with my family may not seem noteworthy, but let me pause for a moment to explain what that meant to the team.

The Thunderbird training season lasts from November through March with a very strenuous schedule of flying and fixing airplanes. All of the new pilots fly two times a day, and some of the second-year pilots fly three times a day to keep the syllabus tracking on schedule. The maintainers work their tails off to keep the jets ready to go, working weekends as necessary to ensure that the planes are ready on Monday. It is a schedule that demands everyone's head be in the game, and there is not a tremendous amount of slack built into the training season. You see, the syllabus requires everyone to progress together to build the final "demonstration" with all six planes during the final weeks of the training season. There are no replacement pilots, so the only pilots who can fly the demonstration for the year are the six who have trained; it is therefore imperative to finish the syllabus on time if the Thunderbird team is going to accomplish its mission for the year beginning in March. With that as context, let me tell you about my team's reaction to the news of my dad's diagnosis.

Boss Mumm said, "Mods, you need to go home and be with your dad for this surgery." It wasn't a question of whether I should go or not, rather a simple scheduling challenge that the team would figure out, so Dianne and I boarded that plane for Buffalo. All of my teammates dove in with prayer support and the simple support of friends who wanted my dad to come through his surgery with flying colors, so the training season for the United States Air Force Demonstration Team slowed to a crawl while I waited with my family outside an operating room in Buffalo. The news was fantastic: the surgery went well, the mass was removed, and the surgeon was upbeat about dad. We visited with him as soon as we were allowed to see him, and he looked really good, considering the ordeal that comprises thoracic surgery. Di and I stayed one more night, visited with my dad again the next day, and, once we were convinced he was on the road to recovery, boarded the plane for Las Vegas and immersion into the training season once again.

1996

The 1996 season was absolutely fantastic for my family in that dad recovered to the point that he was able to play golf in his retirement and he and my mom were able to drive around the East Coast and attend airshows. The first time my dad ever saw the team in person would be when he and my mom attended our airshow in Wilmington, North Carolina. By then, everyone on the team had followed my dad's illness, surgery, and recovery, and all of them welcomed my mom and dad as if they were their own parents. It overwhelmed both of them. John Tobin, our maintenance officer, escorted my mom and dad on one of their days at the show, and the precision and discipline of our team was intoxicating (pun intended) for my father. He absolutely loved everything about the Thunderbirds, including all of the men and women who comprised the team.

As the season wound down in 1996, I was living the American Dream I had envisioned through all those years of night school, all those weekends of studying, and the hard work that goes into being an officer in the United States Air Force. My last entry in my journal captures the essence of the year. I had no idea what 1997 would bring, but I was ready for it, or so I thought.

> *I woke up feeling much better after 11.5 hours sleep.* [I had been feeling sick the day before and had gone to bed at 8:30 PM.] *I had some cereal for breakfast and drank some coffee while reading two papers. Leisurely arrival at work for a 10:30 AM brief and then talked to Dianne for a few minutes before we launched. Uneventful trip to Tinker* [AFB] *against 100+ knots of wind and after a quick lunch, we launched for home. Bigs* [Jeff Fiebig was our slot pilot flying the #4 Jet] *put together a 500 mile Ditty which reminisced through the whole 1996 season, it was great. Our Flex West arrival went well and we were greeted by lots of folks: Dianne, Bill, Sylvia, Barry and Daphne from England, and Reid and Cindy Goodwyn. After we dropped our salute, Poker said "done" as only Poker can, and there were lots of mixed emotions. Scott Ferris seemed sad, and I'm glad we're having them over for dinner. 1996 was a great Thunderbird year; I know as I look back on my life it will be hard to comprehend the whole thing!*

1997

We were two weeks into the 1997 training season when my parents came out to Las Vegas for our Fitzgerald Award banquet and to celebrate Thanksgiving with Di and me. (The Fitzgerald Award was the top enlisted award on the team, as it was given to the enlisted member who most exemplified the hard work, dedication, and selflessness expected of each team member. It was extra special in that the award was given to the winner by his or her peers as they selected the winner from a group of nominations. The award was given in honor of Major Robert Fitzgerald, who was killed in an aircraft accident while the commander/leader of the team in 1961). Mom and Dad had a great time at the banquet, and we all had fun reminiscing about the year and looking forward to 1997. It was at home the next day after my dad was uncharacteristically short about something that he announced he was having headaches. Naturally, we were concerned, and he assured everyone that when he got home, he would see his doctor and have the headaches checked out. We played golf and enjoyed each other's company for the remainder of my parents' visit. When they got home, Dad followed through with his commitment to be seen, only to be given heartbreaking news: The cancer was back in the form of a malignant brain tumor. We were crushed! I immediately reached out to my high school friend and radiologist Champ Summers. He helped us navigate the complex world of medicine, and his professional guidance was awesome for our entire family.

Once again, the team rallied around my family and Di and I hopped back on a plane to Buffalo, almost a year to the day from Dad's lung surgery, to go home and be with my dad for brain surgery. I was absolutely stunned to be able to see my dad in the recovery room just minutes after waking up from his surgery. His head was bandaged and he was wrapped in a thermal blanket; amazingly he was able to sit up and speak with us! It seemed like a miracle as we were once again assured that all the cancer had been removed and that my dad had a seemingly good chance of recovery. We spent another day with my family, visited with Dad in the hospital, and headed back to Nellis to complete the training season. Dad's recovery progressed well, and we started our 1997 show season on April 1. I was staying tuned in to developments at home while taking the Thunderbird mission on the road, and on April 14, I received the news I had been dreading: The cancer was back. I think this point in my life's journey was one of those times as I look back that my faith in God carried me through. I simply focused on taking one day at a time and trusting in God's grace and strength to keep me focused on both my job and my family, and I prayed for the ability to do both. I discussed the path forward for my dad with my mom, my brother and sisters, Dianne, and Champ. It was at this point that I knew my father was going to die. As I type these words, I still become teary eyed thinking about it. Di scheduled herself on a flight for Wednesday at midnight to arrive for the Thursday-morning surgery scheduled for April 17. My family convinced me to remain with the team and to fly to Louisville for our weekend demonstrations and stay tuned to my father's surgery over the phone. After landing at Louisville, I called home to find out my dad was out of surgery and doing well. I said a prayer of thanks and went to work for the weekend.

To say the remainder of the 1997 show season was bittersweet might be the understatement of my life. I was living out my professional dream while the cancer slowly degraded my Fathers condition, but he did recover enough to travel to a few of our shows in 1997. I want to call out two people from my Thunderbird family who exemplified everything good about our team, the Air Force, and America; they are Chief Master Sergeant Joe Baron and Major Loren "Skip" Johnson.

In the summer of 1997, my father was fading fast, but he still wanted to try to travel to see the team in action. On one occasion, he and my mom came to see us in Massachusetts at Hanscom AFB and I had arranged to have quarters on base so we could keep a close eye on dad. When my parents arrived to check in, there had been some confusion, and they had been given a room upstairs though Dad was now too sick to climb stairs. As I was discussing options with the housing folks, I noticed someone behind us who was speaking to someone else and then disappeared only to return with all of his gear. He said "Mods, I've cleared out of my room. Your mom and dad are welcome to it; it's right down the hall." I immediately said no, but Skip dug in and said he absolutely would not go back to his room. Skip had to be moved to another room in another building to find space. I never forgot his act of kindness that day, and I never will.

My father had become very fond of our first sergeant, Joe Baron. We were at the very same show at Hanscom AFB where Skip Johnson had been so kind with his room. The Sleeve, as we called Joe, was as sharp as a tack, and my dad used to say Joe was a "soldier's soldier." The bottom line is that Joe embraced my mom and dad as he embraced his own family, and whenever they were at a show, he volunteered to take care of them in terms of getting them out to show center and back while we briefed our flight, so I asked Joe if he was available to give my mom and dad a lift, and he said, "Absolutely, sir. Where and when do you want me to pick them up?" We coordinated the time and place, and, like always, Joe came through for my mom and dad. It was the next day that I learned a bit about Joe Baron. It turns out that Joe had 10 to 15 of his own family and friends at that airshow and he had to make arrangements to have them taken care of so he could take care of my mom and dad himself. He never said a word to me, nor did he flinch for even a second when asked to help with my parents. I couldn't believe it, but then again when I look at the strength of character in both Joe and Skip, it is easy to believe.

Joe and Skip represent many of the selfless men and women who serve our nation. Their contributions to helping me with my family will never be forgotten and are one of the reasons I believe in the greatness of all Americans. The Thunderbird family is in many ways an extension of all I was raised to believe and value. It was a family that loved one another, was committed to one another, could fight with one another over how to get better, and could then get aligned in terms of reaching a higher standard. It was the most **accountable** organization I have ever seen, and it was truly an honor to serve with all of them.

The Sneak Pass

As I rolled out of my clearing turn, I craned my neck to the right and looked for the diamond. The boss said, "Back right all the way," and I acquired him right where he was supposed to be as he maneuvered the diamond in front of the show line. I gently eased the nose of my fighter over and pushed the throttle to full military power. I would fly a teardrop turn to the right while descending to approximately 125 feet and accelerating to just under the speed of sound. The sneak pass was a crowd favorite and therefore came under great scrutiny by the enlisted members (E's) on the team who expected it to be low, fast, and a total surprise for the crowd. "Nose coming up, rolling left and rolling, diamond ready now," came the boss's call as the diamond executed the Trail to Diamond Roll. This was looking good, and I plugged my afterburner into full power as the boss called, "Nose coming up," for the diamond. Adrenaline flowing, heart pumping fast, breath coming heavy, I had three concerns: Find the 500-foot line from the crowd and get on it, stay below the speed of sound (barely), and don't hit anything (birds, planes, or trees). As the crowd watched the diamond maneuver to the right of show center, my F-16 rocketed past them with a crackle that made people squeal, laugh, and express delight at their American technology and the people sworn to protect them with that technology. It was an honor I shall never forget. At Mach .98, I pulled my beautiful machine into a climbing right turn on my way to 8000 feet above the ground and 20,000 feet away from show center to set up for the High-Low Pass.

A Competitive Spirit

Boys and Their Guardian Angels

One story that explains a bit about my early childhood competitive spirit and my approach to it involved sledding. We had carved a trail down out of some woods near the house, and my cousin Joe, Matt Tuller, and I decided to try it one afternoon. We had a small jump at the bottom of the trail, which permitted us to get "air" going over the bump. I told Joe and Matt that I was going to set a new record and go higher into the woods than ever before. Well, I did. I came down the trail with my hair on fire and was smiling like a Cheshire cat knowing that when I hit that jump, I was going to show Joe and Matt what "real air" looked like. The part I hadn't really thought through was how far I might actually fly. It turns out I flew a long way and landed on my sled so hard, it broke the steering mechanism. I slammed into the metal pole that held up a snow fence that was usually so far away from the normal "landing zone" that we didn't consider it. But with my new record, that post was definitely "in play." The next thing I knew, Joe and Matt were talking over me about the accident and trying to determine whether or not I was OK. They towed me home on a sled and dropped me off with my mom. After 30 minutes of observation, she realized I was going into shock and called the doctor. I was subsequently admitted to the hospital with internal bleeding. It was a three-day stay and another clear indication that all children (especially boys) are given guardian angels to protect us for most of our youth. Thank God for that!

Being Competitive Doesn't Always Mean Winning

One of my most memorable events from my high school years was our West Seneca West homecoming football game senior year. We were up 14–0 with less than 4 minutes to play, and on two long passes, we ended up losing the game 15–14. I was heartbroken. Even as a senior, I welled up with tears as we walked off that field. That competitiveness has always been a part of who I am. My mom and dad attended all of my football games, and my brother, Jeff, would do just about anything to make them as well. I remember that for one game, he drove three hours back from a campsite he was at to watch the game and then drove back to the campsite after the game. He was a competitor himself and loved to play as well as watch competitive activity. My brother said this about me: "Matt was extremely precocious and competitive as a youngster. Dad had to keep a tight rein on him. He hated to lose. Dad would have to say, 'Matt, you can't throw your mitt when you lose.' Matt did not like to lose. He always had a desire to win. That was the influence of our dad."

Following a Call to Service

As school wound down and I contemplated trying to compete and play football at the collegiate level, I all of a sudden had a better idea. Because I really didn't know what I wanted to do in college and had always wanted to fly, I decided to consider enlisting in the Air Force. Although enlisting in the Air Force wouldn't allow me to fly immediately, it would permit me to be around airplanes and see how I liked the military lifestyle. I took the qualifying tests and then broke the news to my parents. They were shocked and, I think, a bit disappointed that I wasn't going to go to college, but they were supportive. My mom recalled, "One day he came into the kitchen and sat down at the table. He told us he didn't want to go to college. He said, 'I want to join the Air Force and I want to fly.' We were floored. He was only seventeen, but quite mature for his age. Matt's father hated to fly, and so do I. But we signed for him so he could join the Air Force." So at seventeen years old, I joined the active duty Air Force and shipped off for basic training on July 29, 1980. Like all new enlistees, I remember that first morning waking up to yelling and screaming by the training instructors (TIs) and thinking, *What the hell have I done?*

I had only been at basic training for a day when the discipline and competitiveness I learned from my father paid off. In our very first inspection by the TIs, I answered the questions they asked crisply and with professionalism. They rewarded that interaction by making me the squad leader and I was the second-youngest member of my unit. I enjoyed the responsibility that came with that leadership opportunity; it would be the first of many times during my Air Force career that my life at home shaped me for the success I would enjoy in the military.

A Perfect Home for a Competitive Spirit

There is no place on earth more competitive than a fighter squadron, and the Thunderbird Squadron was full of 140 Type-A competitors. It was amazing what a clear objective, very high standards, and a relentless commitment to perfection could do when harnessing that competitive spirit. I'm not going to tell you that we never had a squabble, because that would be blatantly false. What I will say is that the competitive spirit that the team has (and that all of the Armed Forces that serve our nation have) was reflected in every person's attention to detail and the fact that they wanted to be as close to perfect as they could be in terms of executing their responsibilities on the team. We never flew a perfect show, or even came close, for that matter. But we never, ever gave up trying to make the next show our first perfect show, and the rest of the squadron exercised their competitive spirit to the same level in whatever job function they had. No wonder we had so much fun executing the mission of the United States Air Force

Thunderbirds! My competitive spirit came to me as one of God's gifts. Americans have always been full of a competitive spirit, and it was a perfect strategic fit for me to find a home serving in the Armed Forces.

The High-Low Pass

I pull heavy breaths on my oxygen mask as I throttle my jet back and look for the diamond 8,000 feet below me in a sweeping right-hand turn. I call, "Five's tally," indicating that I have them visually. I slow down, targeting 250 knots while maintaining my lateral spacing at 20,000 feet from show center. I listen to the boss call out his airspeed and slow the diamond boys down while configuring their jets.

"Gear now" is his command. I watch the diamond roll onto the show line and hear the boss call, "Twelve thousand, two hundred" meaning they are two miles from show center and 200 knots and slowing. This is my cue to begin my portion of the maneuver. I shove the throttle all the way to full military power, roll my fighter on her back, and pull the nose through the horizon and point at the ground. I listen to the boss. "Eight thousand, one-seventy."

I'm late, damn it! I light the afterburner and push forward to maximize the jet's acceleration. Already, I will be downgraded on the maneuver because the beautiful smoke that has been called out by our narrator is gone as my afterburner flame burns it up in the exhaust. The boss calls, "Six thousand," and I pull the power out of afterburner, and begin the fine-tuning that will come at the end of the maneuver. I have the diamond visually, and as the boss makes his 4000 call, I watch the diamond drop into the formation that I will optically "fly right through." The key is to be at the minimum acceptable lateral separation and "stacked appropriately high" to give the people at show center the illusion of flying right through the formation. I listen to the boss call out, "Two thousand," and check my references. It's going to be close. He calls, "One thousand," I power back and sight the show center trailer through the gap in the diamond. "Show center," calls the boss as I fly right through them! It was close; I think I was within 250 feet of show center, and it looked like good optics. I push my throttle to full and wait for the boss's next radio call, which will be my cue to pull nine G's into the vertical and rejoin on the diamond out front of the show line….Oh, how I love this job!

Big Dreams

The Land of Dreams

America has always been a nation that told the world if you have a dream and you're willing to work harder than everyone else who has that same dream, this is a place where you can reach it. From the time I first flew kites and boomerangs off the hill in front of my house in rural East Chatham, New York, I told my family that someday I wanted to fly jets. No one in my family had flown anywhere in their lives, but in America, that doesn't matter. No one in my family ever said, "Oh, Matt, that's not possible for you." I am grateful for the never-ending support of my family. One of the realities I have witnessed is that most people don't dream big enough. One of the other realities that we are seeing today in America is that we have confused the basic promise that the country offers, which is equal opportunity, with something that's never been promised which is equal results. The hard work part of turning a dream into reality cannot be minimized, but if one is pursuing a dream versus simply trudging through life, it's a lot easier to work hard. There are plenty of people who will try to limit the dreams we have based on their own preconceived biases and limited thinking; I have characterized these folks "dream disablers." They are the ones who tell you, "That's too hard," "You're too small," or "You're too dumb." All through my life's journey, I have found the ratio of dream disablers to dream enablers to be heavily skewed in favor of the number of disablers. Dream enablers are those people in life who simply want to help you achieve your dreams and who are committed to that end. I have always sought out dream enablers and have tried my best to be one for all of the people I lead, including my children. Reflect on the best boss, best leader, or other most influential people in your life. Many of them will fit the mold of dream enablers. Dream enablers can affect our lives at the core and can affect our lives in pursuit of our actual dreams. I'll share examples of both throughout my life.

Boyhood Dream Enablers

Mr. Burkhardt was our wonderful and patient neighbor in East Chatham, and he had an old barn with all sorts of neat old things in it: cars, mowers, antique machinery…it was a busy boy's paradise. One year in the spring—I must have been seven or eight—Mr. Burkhardt let me help him take an old mower apart to free a sticking valve. He patiently taught me each step of the process and let me use the tools. I was so proud when we finished, put gas in it, and had it start right up when we pulled the string. It was the following year that I really learned something about Mr. Burkhardt and about the pride that comes with accomplishment. The following spring, the old mower had been sitting all winter and the valve was stuck again. I asked Mr. Burkhardt if I could help him fix it. He looked me square in the eye and said, "You fixed it last year. There are the tools; go ahead and fix it." I was astonished that he was going to let me work on that old mower all by myself, because my track record for getting things back together in working order was significantly less than 100%. I have never forgotten how I felt when I wound up that old string on the mower and pulled it and the mower started right up after I had put it back together all by myself. The fact that I am nearing 50 years old and that typing these words still brings a tingle to the back of my neck tells you the impact that this one incident had on my formation as a young man. We need to know and believe that we can accomplish whatever we set out to accomplish, and we all need more Mr. Burkhardts in our lives, because they are our dream enablers!

Thunderbird Dream is Born

Right after I arrived at Reese AFB outside Lubbock, Texas, I was inspired by my jet engine trainer, Roger Henry. Roger had gone to the Thunderbirds as a mechanic, and when he described the environment of the team, I made up my mind that ultimately, I wanted to fly as a demonstration pilot for the USAF Thunderbirds. Never mind that in the history of the Air Force (in 1980), there had been fewer than 100 people who had been honored to serve in that capacity. I now had a dream, and my first step to accomplishing that dream was the need for a college education. I applied for and was awarded a Reserve Officer Training Corp (ROTC) scholarship that would permit me to pursue college full time and then return to the Air Force as an officer. The first major setback to my plans was a letter that I received from the ROTC medical review board that stated I was not pilot qualified for eyesight. When I opened the letter on my dorm room bed, I lay down and cried. My roommate, Dennis Nelson, came in and thought someone had died in my family. I was devastated!

Years later, I would come to believe that this particular detour in my journey was actually a needed developmental twist and all part of the plan. Without my time as an air traffic controller, my ultimate success in pilot training and the world of flying Air Force fighters would have been diminished for two main reasons. The first reason is that I never learned to study or fully commit myself until I attended air traffic control school, and I needed that discipline later in flight school. Second, knowing what the air traffic controllers want you to do while flying along at 420 knots in a T-38 gives a student a huge advantage in situational awareness, and that edge was also important in my pilot training success.

Dream Enablers Continued

When I met the minimum requirements to apply for the Thunderbird Team, I put in an application and got the "Dear Matt" letter from Thunderbird One, Boss Andersen: "Dear Matt, you have an exemplary record.....blah, blah, blah, keep up the great work." All I knew was that I didn't make the first cut.

Lieutenant Colonel Paul "Snoopy" Schafer asked me, "Mods, why didn't you make the team? What was the feedback?" I told him that the only feedback I had been able to obtain was that my total flying time was less than the team would like. He said, "Well then, let's get you all the time we can between now and next year's application." When scheduling fighter missions, there are only so many ways to beef up one's hours: You can fly more missions, or you can fly longer missions. Lieutenant Colonel Schafer helped me do both.

Davis-Monthan was an A-10 training base, meaning our training missions there were fairly scripted with new students. The entire syllabus consisted of many different areas of training where the students needed to complete a certain number of flying events to graduate from the school. Lieutenant Colonel Schafer told me that when the students I was flying with completed their mission requirements, I could drop them off (we were in different airplanes, as all of the A-10s were single seat) and then continue flying instrument approaches for my own currency and to build my hours 15 minutes at a time. He also scheduled me to fly other missions like ferrying jets to depot for maintenance or dropping off spare parts for broken jets that were stuck at out bases. The bottom line is this: I flew as often as the schedule would allow during the next year in Lieutenant Colonel Paul Schafer's 357th Fighter Squadron, and my boss helped me build my time at every possible opportunity. When the time rolled around for me to apply for the team again, my hours were 50 to 100 more than they would have been without his help.

Lieutenant Colonel Schafer was a dream enabler, and he helped me eliminate barriers to successfully competing for a chance to fulfill my dream. He was also one of the finest leaders I ever had the chance to work for during my Air Force career and now serves our nation and our Air Force in the rank of major general.

Cadillac Dreams of My Father

My father grew up in a tough climate. His mother died when he was 12, and his dad was a tough man who eventually remarried and had two more children with his new wife. My father was expected to work hard, and he learned his work ethic from his own dad. Because he grew up in a very modest family, my father *never* owned a new car his entire life. He thought they were a horrible investment (he was right), and he always had his "next car" picked out based on people he knew who took care of their cars and then sold them to buy new. My dad had a standing joke based on this habit of buying old cars. He'd always say, "Someday when I get my Cadillac," and then finish his thought. He never really expected or probably even desired a new Cadillac, but the idea of wishing for one out loud became a family joke of ours for years.

When Dianne and I moved back from England and landed in Tucson, I was amazed at life in the desert. The weather was perfect for flying fighters (unlike England): It was hot, the creatures that lived there had bad bites (scorpions and rattlesnakes), and the cars had no rust. When you come from Buffalo, this seems strange. It was this last point that had my attention as my father announced his intention to retire from a life in the utility company at the age of 62. I thought, *What if we could find an old Cadillac for Dad, fix it up, and give it to him for his retirement present? How cool would that be?* I brought the idea to my family, and they told me I was nuts. I then brought the idea to Dianne, who told me I was nuts but that she would support the search and the mission if we could find one for the right price. Well, I found it, and we bought a 1976 Cadillac Sedan Deville with a huge V-8 engine and the need for lots of TLC for $1600.00.

Dianne then lived with "Big Blue" being the sole occupant of our garage for months as I tore off all of the chrome and polished it, fixed small problems, had the vinyl top replaced, and then painted the car in the base hobby shop at Davis-Monthan AFB (twice because I screwed up the first paint job).

When my parents came down to visit us in the winter, we were ready to present Dad with his new retirement gift, his Cadillac! I hadn't seen my dad mist up too many times in life, but we got him with the Cadillac, and he was as proud of that old thing as of any other car he had ever owned. I was proud that I could help him enjoy one small "dream" in life for all he'd done for us through the years. My parents had driven a rental car down to see us and as such had to arrange to get Big Blue delivered to their home in western New York on a flatbed truck. She looked cold coming off the truck all covered with ice and snow, but Big Blue had a very proud new owner. Blue got about eight miles per gallon, and my dad jokingly said many times afterward that "It's a good thing that car was free, because the gas would have broken my bank account." That's my dad and the story of his Cadillac dream.

Reaching My Dream

The whirlwind began one afternoon in the 357th Fighter Squadron in Tucson, Arizona, when the squadron intercom system boomed, "Captain Modleski, Thunderbird One is on the phone and wants to speak with you." I was more nervous getting to that phone that at any other time in the Thunderbird application process because I knew one way or the other that I was going to find out the fate of a dream that had begun 15 years prior to picking up that receiver. As I settled into a chair in one of the squadron offices, several of my friends peeked around the corner of the doorframe, waiting to hear one way or the other.

I said, "Captain Modleski. May I help you?"

Lieutenant Colonel Andersen, the current boss of the team, said simply, "Hi, Mods. Boss Andersen here. How'd you like to be the opposing solo on next year's team?"

I can't even remember all that I said in response. I hope it was professional and courteous, but I know for sure some of the words were "Yes, sir, it would be an honor." We talked for a minute or two about logistics, F-16 school, timelines, and the like, and then we hung up. I can't describe the feeling I had over being given the chance to join what I had always considered America's team (sorry, Cowboys fans). I called Dianne immediately after hugging several of my squadron mates as they lined up to say congratulations, then I called home to share the news with my family. Dianne and I were so honored to represent America and the Air Force in service to the nation that to be headed for the Thunderbirds to serve seemed almost like a dream, an impossible reality, now that it had actually happened. Truth be told, I think we were a bit numbed by it all for a few days.

As with most military families, the planning began almost immediately. Our home went on the market, and we went to Las Vegas to find a new home there. I prepared to leave my current job as a flight commander in the 357th and take on the role of student in an F-16 squadron at Luke AFB in Phoenix. As we prepared for the transition to a very fast-paced two and a half years, Dianne as always had the hardest job. Not only was she working as a nurse, but she would have to keep the house ready to show at all times and do all of the preliminary packing. With our golden retriever, Chatham, that meant daily vacuuming, along with all of the other household chores. Last but not least, she would have to relocate her career once again and find new jobs, both as a civilian and as a reserve officer in the Air Force nursing corps.

With all of that activity swirling, I headed for Luke AFB to begin training in the F-16. The course for transitioning Thunderbird pilots is a somewhat abbreviated course because employing the airplane in combat is not part of the Thunderbirds' mission. I met my new boss when I arrived at Luke, and he and I went out for dinner on our first night there together. His name was Ron Mumm, and his call sign was Maxi. Boss Mumm was an easygoing Southern fellow who picked up early on the fact that I was a Yankee and who teased me about all sorts of stuff. We hit it off relatively quickly, and I enjoyed spending time getting to know him and learning to fly the F-16 with him. Maxi had come out of the F-15, so he needed to learn the F-16 just as I did, but his knowledge of things like radar and air-to-air maneuvering was much more advanced than mine because I was coming out of the mighty Warthog.

I learned quickly that I had to ask Boss Mumm before accepting a dinner invitation whether we were going out "to eat" or "to dine." Normally, I needed more time at the books than he did to fully prepare for the next day's academics or mission, and Boss Mumm loved to dine. Eating took 30 to 60 minutes, but dining could take up to three or four hours, start to finish. We still joke about it to this day. We used that time together to become better teammates. I would come to believe that being the commander/leader of the USAF Thunderbirds was the hardest peacetime job in the Air Force; I still believe that to this day. Find me another squadron commander who flies 10 to 15 times a week, gets critiqued mercilessly by those who fly with him, answers phone calls from his own generals as well as any others who might choose to pick up the phone and call him, and has to always be "on" when dealing with everyone who interacts with the team. I may change my mind if you can find such a job; otherwise, I still believe that being Thunderbird One is the toughest peacetime Squadron Commander job in the Air Force.

Boss Mumm and I finished up F-16 school in October 1995 and headed for Las Vegas to join the team. Dianne, as she always did, organized everything for our move to a T. We sold the house in Tucson and found a new one in North Las Vegas, and she found a great job as a nurse in Vegas and as a reservist on base. We were ready to go, so we packed up our golden retriever (he was probably happy to leave, having been bitten by both a rattlesnake and a scorpion), said good-bye to the very first home that we had owned, and headed for sunny Las Vegas and the start of the fastest assignment of our lives!

Dreams—Our Boys

Most of my early childhood was spent outside enjoying every day as if it was the best day ever and believing anything was possible even though we were a very middle-class family in East Chatham, New York. I see that same exuberance in my boys now, and I love the way they approach life. I hope the pace of life, the crazy level of activity that 2011 brings to us, never dims their enthusiasm for today, the next great day in their lives. Our "team objective" with the boys is to ensure that they grow up to be fine young men (if you ask my fourth–grader, he'll tell you that's our objective). As a father, strategist, and dreamer myself, I want to ensure that we help them identify their core strengths and God's gifts and that we give them every opportunity we can for them to be successful using those gifts. Keaton has been blessed with curiosity, energy, a good brain for math, and a competitiveness that will serve him well in athletics and beyond (if we can round a few sharp edges). Jacob loves people and really loves to talk with everyone, as verbal skills have always been at his core. He is a good athlete and shares some of the competitive spirit that his brother has in buckets.

Our boys should always believe that in America, if you'll outwork others who compete with you and work alongside others who dream with you, anything is possible. They are a reminder every day of how we should approach life and its challenges, happy to be here and giving everything we do our full effort. Oh, how we love our boys!

Keaton

Jacob

Perseverance

Learning to Commit 100%

When I cross-trained (switched jobs using an Air Force career-management program) into air traffic control from the jet engine career field, my life changed dramatically and forever. It was the time in my young adult life when I learned the value of 100% commitment and the results that can be achieved with that level of focus. Air traffic control school was renowned for its high failure rate, so the dream disablers came out in full force when I announced my intentions to attend the school. Undeterred, I headed for Keesler AFB in Biloxi, Mississippi, to begin my training. As fate would have it, my class dates extended over the Christmas and New Year holidays and the school shut down for 12 days. I decided to forego the trip home to be with family and instead committed to studying for eight full hours every day of that break. I had never displayed that type of rigor in terms of my own commitment to academics, and I learned that with that type of commitment and effort, nearly anything would be possible in life. I graduated with the highest average the school had ever produced, a 99.25%, and this from the same kid who had barely passed his high school chemistry final with a 65%.

One of the requirements for air traffic controllers is to have an annual flight physical. I was in one of those physicals when I asked the question that would ultimately change my life's direction and reignite a dormant dream. I was sitting in the optometrist's chair at Dover AFB, Delaware, and I asked, "Doctor, what's wrong with my eyes that makes me disqualified for flight training?" As a young airman, I had never been fully detailed on why I failed the ROTC physical, and the paperwork had simply said, "Refractor error outside acceptable limits."

This doctor looked me right in the eye and said, "There's nothing wrong with your eyes. I'd give you a Class I physical right now." That meant I was qualified for pilot training! I wanted to hug him! It turns out that astigmatisms can cause refractor error and can modulate in their severity. No matter how it happened, I had been given news that changed my life.

Once I learned that my eyes were indeed good enough to apply to USAF pilot training, I attended night school with a vengeance. I also learned to fly in my free time and along the way met and married Dianne, my wife of 23 years. I was dating Di when I applied to officer training school (OTS) for the first time, and she was there to support me when I was summarily rejected. No one knew why I wasn't selected by the OTS board; then again, no one really knew how my refractor error had fixed itself, either. When the next OTS selection board met, I was accepted. This forced the wedding Di and I had been planning (actually, Di and her mother had been planning) for December all the way forward to August, and it was already May. We had a beautiful wedding (thanks, Mom and Dad Reilly), and I headed for OTS in San Antonio.

The Hog Flight Path

Undergraduate pilot training is a long year of hard work, but the rewards are earning the wings of a USAF pilot. The assignment process is a mix of objective and subjective measures resulting in everyone being ranked from first in the class to the last person in the class (similar to medical school, the last person in the med school class is called "doctor" and the last person in the pilot training class is called a "pilot"). It was a great honor for a student to simply earn wings, as approximately 30% of the class didn't finish and were sent home or off to other career fields. It was a competitive environment because, typically, the top 10% of the class received their "choice of airplane" and from that point on, their aviation career tracks would be set. In what turned out to be the only time this had happened in anyone's memory, I was honored as our class' top graduate and received my fourth choice of airplane, the A-10 Warthog. Sometimes it's hard to see the forest for the trees, and although I was thrilled to be going into fighter aviation, the Hog was slow, ugly, and not the plane that the Thunderbirds flew. It turned out to be the best assignment that I could have ever received, however, and as a result, I had a chance to do many things earlier than I could have in another weapons system. I mention some of those things in "Hog Facts" under "Accountability!"

Over-Prepared for the Interview of a Lifetime

"I'll have the interview of a lifetime." That's what I thought when I was notified that I was a semifinalist for selection to the team in the spring of 1995 and was informed that part of the process was a formal job interview. The only significant problem was I'd never had to formally interview for anything because I'd been in the Air Force my whole adult life, so I got to work.

I read a couple of books on interviewing and listened to a third book on tape. The key take-away from all of that work was this: have a plan to control the interview. That made sense to me, so I looked at the mission of the Thunderbird team, and from that, I pulled the key elements that encapsulated the reason the team exists: "to recruit and retain members of the Air Force and to inspire and motivate those same members as well as all Americans and our international friends." Those criteria were the basis for my planning. I then set about thinking of my competition. The other semifinalists all flew pointy-nosed fast jets—F-16s or F-15s—and I flew the A-10, a slow-moving Warthog. That was neither a strength nor an insurmountable weakness, but I needed to find a way to differentiate myself uniquely, and focusing on the team's mission was where I found my best source of competitive advantage.

When I looked at those mission elements of "recruiting and retaining, inspiring and motivating" and I looked at my background, I saw the way to differentiate myself: my Air Force story. I had enlisted at 17 years old, cross-trained into a second career, gone to school at night for both my bachelor's degree and my master's degree, and become an officer and fighter pilot, **all by using Air Force**

programs. What better way to recruit and retain, inspire and motivate than to have a walking, talking example of how all of those programs could be utilized to ultimately achieve a dream of flying jet fighters and fly them on the USAF Thunderbirds? I had my differentiator and now had to decide how best to prepare.

In some of my research on interviewing, I had come across several iterations of commonly asked interview questions. I took the top questions I could find plus found some people who had previously interviewed with the team and asked them if they remembered any questions from their interviews. I wrote out my answers to all of those questions (approaching 100 of them), answering them from a personal perspective as well as a professional perspective, and always, where possible, I linked them back to my Air Force story, my real uniqueness or strategy.

I had no computer in 1995 (yet), so I did all of this in pencil and longhand. I then began to practice the answers to the questions by reading the questions from paper and then practicing my responses while trying not to look at the answer. Over and over I did this, until I had rehearsed the answers and knew what I wanted to say. I then got out my video camera and asked and answered the questions on film, and then I studied the film to see how I looked and sounded. After getting myself to a satisfactory point, I had my wife ask me the questions and I practiced my answers and studied the film. Then I had my good friend Lance Schroeder ask me the questions, and I studied the film. I also asked Lance for his candid feedback in terms of the message I was trying to convey and what he perceived as he listened to my answers. If he wasn't hearing what I thought I was saying, I reconsidered the words I was using

to deliver my intended message. Once all of that preparation was finished, my final step was to grab an acquain-
tance from the squadron and have him ask me the
questions and see how I answered them under that additional pressure of not really being close to the questioner.
I can't even remember who asked me the questions, to be
honest, but that was my final test. After looking at that
film, I simply continued to review my questions and
answers and felt fully prepared for my "interview of a lifetime"! Tony Seely remembered this about my interview
experience:

>At the interview process we were all in the
>room. The appies [what the team members
>call the applicants for the team] wait outside
>while the interviewee in the room wraps up.
>Normally, no one messes with an appie because
>you know they're nervous. But we all knew
>Matt was going to be great. Just after we
>stepped out into the hallway to give Matt a
>time back [for example, "It's ten–twenty-
>two. Your interview starts in thirty-five
>seconds."]—precision is everything on the
>team—our announcer, J.K. Switzer, jumped
>up and locked the door.

>The next thing we know, there's a knock
>on the door in precisely 35 seconds. "Sir, the
>door appears to be locked." That was Matt. It
>was funny. He was king. He overcame. I
>didn't know he had practiced in front of a video
>camera for eighty hours, but it paid off. He
>blew everyone's socks off.

Accountability

Boyhood Accountability—A Requirement for Success

I learned a hard lesson about accountability when I was no more than six or seven years old. Ricky Klinger and I (always in trouble when we were together) began tossing around the backyard a doll that a friend of ours had left behind when she went home. The tossing got rougher and rougher until at last there simply wasn't much left of the doll. We put the broken pieces under our sun porch (a type of burial, I suppose) but my mother soon discovered the crime scene and all the evidence. Of course by the time of discovery, Ricky was long gone and I was left to accept accountability for my actions alone. My mom made me take all the pieces of that doll and carry them up to the little girl's house. Through blubbering tears, I explained that I was the one who had destroyed her doll and I apologized to both the girl and her mom. I'll never forget how that felt or will I forget that the girl and her mom both forgave me and invited me in for a piece of cake.

One of the reasons I thrived in the military was the fact that there was accountability. My father was a tough man, but he taught us right from wrong, and he also reinforced consequences for our decisions. The military further reinforced those lessons and rewarded people who could take accountability for their actions and accomplish the mission along the way.

Hog Facts

Aviation in general is a very accountable business. Training is tightly managed, and clear standards and objectives must be met to maintain proficiency and currency. In a fighter squadron, add competition to those exacting standards, and what you get is a factory of accountability. When I first came to the A-10, I had mixed emotions, as the airplane isn't what you'd call a sexy fighter. The first time I pulled the trigger and shot the gun, all of that changed and I became enamored with all the airplane could do...and do very well.

I went through A-10 training in Tucson, Arizona, and eventually came back to Tucson as an instructor pilot in the 357th Fighter Squadron, the Dragons. But my first A-10 assignment in the United Kingdom at RAF Bentwaters/Woodbridge was where I learned accountability fighter-pilot style and the value of accountability when problem-solving.

The first lesson in fighter aviation is to set clear objectives. The only way we can know whether we are improving the skills required to defend the nation and have the right strategy and tactics to accomplish anything is to set very clear measurable objectives and then hold one another accountable to them. This accountability came in the form of a debrief in the fighter world, where the clear objectives for the mission were restated and put up on a board for all to see, and then every member of the team held himself or herself accountable for accomplishing his or her portion of the mission. Sometimes these discussions would get quite heated, and rank had no place in the debrief. The flight leader (the person assigned overall responsibility for the planning and execution of the mission) ran the debrief, and many times, flight members of higher rank would be "corrected" in terms of their performance with no regard for their rank. It was a great example of accountability well executed for the good of the mission, the team, and the nation. "Growing up" in the A-10 world afforded me the chance to grow faster than some other weapons systems would have allowed me to, and I was a flight-lead, instructor pilot, and even an evaluator pilot all while still a lieutenant. I loved the environment, I loved my squadron mates, I loved the competition, and I loved serving the nation as an Air Force officer and A-10 pilot.

Thunderbird Accountability

There is only one fighter squadron in the Air Force in which the pilot skips his/her preflight inspection and then straps the jet on and flies an inverted pass at 125 feet off the ground at nearly 500 miles per hour—the Thunderbird Squadron. Aviation is a very accountable business because the consequences for being unaccountable are so great. One of the things I used to love telling high school kids when we spoke to them was "I trust my crew chiefs with my life, literally!" I could see them sit up a bit straighter and see many of them think, *That's cool. I wonder if I could do that?* Accountability is a distinctly American value that the founders of our nation understood as they risked everything they had to fight for freedom. It is an area we'll spend more time on in part two of this book.

Service that Shapes Accountability in a Man

I was a young noncommissioned officer (NCO) who had found success in the Air Force, enjoyed the life and career I had begun, and thought I had a pretty good picture of what "service to country" meant. All that changed with one additional duty assignment.

As many of you know, Dover AFB is the base in the US that receives the Remains of our fallen warriors. What many probably don't know is that whenever the Remains of a fallen service member are sent home to his or her family, an escort is assigned to help facilitate every facet of the military honors that are due that warrior. The escort also helps to coordinate and navigate all of the details that have to be dealt with any time government red tape is involved.

In August 1985, terrorism was still something that seemed to "happen over there" for most Americans. A car bomb went off at Rhein Mein AB in Germany, and two people were killed: Airman Frank H. Scarton, 19 years old, of Woodhaven, Michigan, and a civilian woman named Becky Jo Bristol of San Antonio. My phone rang, and I was summoned to the squadron and told that I would receive some training on the protocol involved and then I was to take the body of Frank Scarton back to his wife and high school sweetheart, Mary, and his grieving family. I was a bit shocked, nervous, and, at the same time, honored to be selected for such an assignment. I had no idea what to expect. In the interest of the family's privacy, I am simply going to say this about meeting all of them under such stressful circumstances: They were proud Americans who had given a loved one to serve our nation, and their loved one Frank paid the ultimate price in defense of America. I have never been more proud to wear the uniform than on those days when I represented the United States Air Force for a family who had given so much to us and I came to care for them as if they were my own family. The experience changed my life forever, and I never viewed my work in the Air Force again as a job. It was a vocation, and one that deserved a bit more respect than I had been giving it.

I learned that being a professional NCO meant more than being a good air traffic controller, and I learned that wearing the uniform with extreme pride wasn't done just because we had a regulation (AFR 35-10) that said we had to, it was part of being a professional airman. What I learned was that no matter where I wore that uniform, someone who had given just as much as the Scarton family might be watching me and expecting me to show the respect their loved one had earned for the uniform and our country. I don't believe after the honor of escorting Frank home that I ever forgot that lesson.

Mary and I have exchanged Christmas cards for 25 years, but before communicating this story in this book, I decided to reach out to Mary to ensure that she was okay with bringing the story to print after all of these years. In June 2010, Mary and I spoke after 25 years, and I am proud to say she has grown to be the proud mother of two beautiful children. She is as proud of America today as she has ever been, though she has many of the same concerns that all of us have for our country. It was wonderful to catch up with Mary and fill in the years, and she succinctly stated when we were speaking with one another, "You should include this story in your book. After all, it shaped both of our lives in a very real way." Mary, you are oh so right!

Faith

Mom's Wisdom—If You Can, Find a Better Way

It has been said many times that there are no atheists in foxholes; let me add there aren't many at basic military training either. I was raised as a Sunday-Mass Catholic. We practiced many of the sacraments but selectively skipped many others; the one aspect of my faith that was clearly etched in my brain was the belief in God. I had the same questions all teens have about why bad things happen and how there could be an ever-present God. All of my questions and challenges to my faith were simply a result of my desire to understand with a human mind the things that are simply beyond comprehension and actually require faith. I remember during one of my more rambunctious rants with my mom about God and Jesus and good and evil that my mom stopped me and said, **"Matthew, if you can find a better way to live your life than the way Jesus taught us, then go ahead and do it; otherwise, it's a pretty good template for the way to live."** Through all of my ups and downs, my successes and failures in life and in my faith, I have always come back to Mom's wisdom and realized she was right.

I had only been at OTS for a few days when I really was questioning whether I wanted to stay. I had been married to Dianne for five weeks before driving down to San Antonio for OTS, and on the way, I was in a bad car crash. I had been driving for 11 hours, and it was raining very hard. As I crested a hill on I-85, I was met with taillights and stopped traffic. An accident at the bottom of the hill had the traffic backed up to a stop all the way to the top of the hill. I hit the brakes as hard as I could, and as I realized

I might not be able to stop, I headed for the shoulder of the road. At that point, a car went zipping past me on the median, and mud and dirt were flying everywhere. Just then, I was thinking about looking in my mirror to see if the car behind him was going to stop, and BAM! I was rear-ended by a fellow who barely had touched his brakes! I went back to Dover with the help of a good Samaritan tow truck driver who really was an angel in coveralls. When I packed my car for the trip, I had laid all my uniforms flat in the back so they wouldn't get wrinkled on the way to OTS. Therefore I had no luggage! The good Samaritan helped me get all my things out of my car and took me to buy luggage for those clothes. Finally, he took me to the airport to catch a flight back to Dover. I've never forgotten the kindness of that American. At Dover, I was examined by the flight surgeon on base and was cleared to fly down to San Antonio to attend OTS.

Once I was at OTS, the bottom line was that my neck hurt, I missed my wife, and I could think of a lot of things I'd rather be doing than getting bossed around by the six-week wonders who were running the school as the upper class. OTS simulates the process used in the military academies in that the entire school is used as a leadership laboratory. At the halfway point in the curriculum, the lower class assumes the leadership roles in the school and begins to lead the new lower classmen. I found myself in the OTS chapel, asking God to guide my decision-making and to let me be true to the path I was supposed to be on in life. My family was all very supportive during that first week and told me they'd love me no matter what I did. They encouraged me to realize I was living out a dream that I had talked about my whole life. They lovingly cautioned me about making decisions while I was still emotional about several aspects of my life. The long story short is this: I stayed, led our squadron from last place to first, and finished as the top graduate in my class, but not without a reliance on my faith.

Saying Good-Bye to My Father

In September 1997, I saw my father for the last time in my parents' home in West Seneca, New York. Dianne and I had driven back from Syracuse, where the team was performing for the weekend; we had spent the night, and it was time to go. I was dressed in my show suit, and I gave Dad a hug in his hospital bed in my parents' home and told him I loved him. It was faith that permitted me to leave Dad and fly an airshow with focus that afternoon. I fully expected to see my dad at Thanksgiving two months later, but that was not to be. When my father had been diagnosed with lung cancer in my first few months on the Thunderbirds, it had been devastating for our family. We had been nervous, anxious, and worried for the health of my dad. It was another time that God had been waiting there for me when I needed Him. Flying around at 125 feet, upside down and at 500 knots is not the time to be unfocused, and my faith was my foundation. When my father recovered completely for the 1996 show season, a year my mom calls the best in our family's history, it was those many prayers answered. My father enjoyed so much the discipline and precision of our team, and it truly was a gift from God that he had a chance to be there to enjoy it. My Thunderbird teammates had rallied around my family, and my family had been treated like all of the families were—as if they were the most important family at the show. The cancer returned and eventually took my father's life on November 22, 1997. My father died on the evening that we officially welcomed the new officers to the team and I passed the torch to my replacement. In the words of astronaut Charlie Duke in his book *Moonwalker*, it was another of the many "God Incidences" (versus coincidences) in my life.

Footprints in the Sand

One of my favorite poems is the famous "Footprints in the Sand," made very popular by Mary Stevenson. In the poem, a person is walking with Jesus, and they look back together at the person's life and the two sets of footprints in the sand that represent Jesus being with the person for life's journey. With a bit of indignation, the person asks, "during the most trying periods of my life there have been only one set of footprints in the sand. Why, when I needed you most, have you not been there for me?" Jesus says to the person, "The times when you have seen only one set of footprints, is when I carried you."

In my lowest points in life, God has been there for me, and the words of my mom resonate in my head often. Our family is more grounded in our faith than I was as a youngster, and I hope my boys ask the same hard questions that I did as they grow and mature and learn the world around them. They already have heard the answer that they will get from me (my mom's answer), and they believe as I do that there is indeed a God Almighty, maker of heaven and earth. It is our ability to live the way He demands, and that his Son, Jesus, reinforced, that will ultimately grade out our lives here on earth; everything else is just noise.

There is no better way to display the role that faith played for me during my two years on the Thunderbirds than to copy the last page (verbatim) from the journal I kept in 1997

> *Reflections: Well, my Thunderbird era has come to a close, and 1997 was a good T-bird year. The 50th anniversary of the Air Force was wonderful, and to be on the team was equally wonderful. I'm proud of Dianne for all her support during a personally challenging year for me. I could have never made it through without all her effort; I need to make sure she knows that. There were lots of frustrations at the pace of decisions and the inconsistency between some of those decisions, but that's life. The fact is, the mission of the Thunderbirds is to give. To give pride, inspiration, and magic to all those Americans who really need the things we give. I've given all I could. I know I could have probably done more in some areas, but I'm proud of my contributions to our team. This year will always be double-edged, one of my best and one of my worst. As Dad fades from this life and moves to the next one, I know he was proud of me and especially proud of our team. It's been tough for the family, but we will survive and we will be strong. Good-bye to this first dream I've accomplished, and may it only be the start of a future so bright. Good-bye to my dad, who fought so long and hard to make it through the show season. He did it—thank him and thank God!*

PART TWO

What We Must Do to Secure Our Children's Dreams

America has proven to be an awesome nation—not free of faults, but full of the possibility to dream and accomplish one's goals. Our founding fathers clearly knew of the risks to a nation based on individual freedom free of accountability. It's why they spoke of God so often. Although there are some who don't believe in God, there are many more of us who do. The beauty in America is that we are free to believe as we wish, but behavior with fewer moral boundaries has led us to where we are today, and I ask you, "How's that working for us?" It is not enough to have the moral compass that comes with strong faith; the challenge for us going forward is to make better use of that compass in the way we live our lives.

I believe we have the courage to pull ourselves up by the bootstraps as we have in the past and to find leaders who will serve for the good of the nation rather than for individual interests, but we have to take on the challenge.

My purpose in this part of the book is to generate meaningful dialogue that gets us together to begin the hard work on the path forward for our great nation; and to do it with a realistic view of what's going to be required.

How Did We Get Here?

One of the best things I learned as a competitive fighter pilot was to look at the big picture before worrying about the smaller picture. It is from that more strategic view that we often find our best solutions to problems on the strategic level, not the tactical one. When I retired from the Air Force, I decided to open a small business, and soon after beginning my adventure, my wife announced she was pregnant with our first son, Keaton. It was fantastic news and required a career change, as the cost of living in Illinois surpassed my new business' earning power and Dianne wanted to move from her full-time employment to part-time status, a move that I wholeheartedly endorsed. The long and the short of it is that I ended up in the world of healthcare, working for Roche Diagnostics for nearly five years. I've now been in the healthcare marketplace for nearly ten years, the last 5 as a partner in a small consulting firm, Stovall Grainger Modleski, that teaches the application of strategy in business.

As a company that focuses on teaching the application of strategy in the healthcare marketplace, it is the big-picture view of what's happened in America, both in healthcare and in nearly every facet of society that has motivated me to write this book. I wrote the first half of the book to provide you a chance to get to know me and a bit more about my journey to the USAF Thunderbirds. I think before reading anyone's perspective on the challenges we face as a nation, one should know where that perspective comes from and how it was shaped. This second part of the book attempts to look at several of our most challenging problems from a high level and to lay out the truth in how we arrived here. It will involve looking in the mirror, and my goal here is to put the challenges in front of us, all Americans, for discussion and action. As a career strategist and consultant who spends time helping organizations compete more effectively, when I work with a client, I always make them articulate a specific, measurable, attainable, realistic, and time-bound (SMART) objective. It is my hope that with some clarity and tough discussions amongst ourselves as Americans, we might begin to send people to Washington who are courageous enough to listen to our concerns and articulate their objectives in SMART terms; the future of our nation depends on it.

If You're Not Growing, You're Dying

Dr. George Land wrote a book called *Grow or Die*. In it, he articulates the fact that any entity is perpetually in one of three phases of growth: formative, normative, or integrative, or, as we simply teach our clients, Phase I, II, or III. When we apply Dr. Land's work to our course in teaching strategy, we typically apply it to people and businesses. It applies to nations as well, however.

Within each of the three phases of growth, many characteristics are common, regardless of whether we are talking about individuals, businesses, or nations. For the purposes of our discussion, let's focus on two business examples from the past and then let's talk about our country.

When we talk about a business in Phase I growth (see illustration on page 72) there are some really cool things happening. Innovation and creativity are alive. Someone has a great idea, and there is a tremendous amount of energy around that idea. The productivity in Phase I is minimal, as the idea has to be developed and grown into maturity, which happens in Phase II. In terms of businesses, let's use Polaroid and IBM as our two examples. In terms of our nation, let's focus on the cycle of growth that's taken place since WWII ended which is when our ascent to the manufacturing leader of the world began. Let's look at how it has played out in Phase II of the growth curve.

Polaroid had the great idea to bring pictures to life instantly. In Phase I, this was simply an idea with rather poor technology (remember the first instant pictures), but Polaroid knew that instant pictures would succeed if they could just make the improvements necessary to their product. They launched what turned out to be paradigm-shifting technology in the film world and went on to make an enormous amount of money in the process. All of the process improvement, refinement of technology, and money making take place during Phase II of a business's growth cycle, but with all that success come a few challenges. Characteristics described by words like complacent, stagnant, self-absorbed, and lazy begin to creep into the psyche of an organization whose success is undeniable in Phase II, and the organization becomes vulnerable to what we call a strategic inflection point. If you look at the growth curve at the top of Phase II, you see that something happens to begin to curtail that growth. It is at that point in time that the rules of the game have changed. No one gets to solely determine when these inflection points happen, but when the changes happen, the old rules won't work. The new paradigm is being established by a new player with a different set of rules. This is where non-strategic, overconfident businesses fail. How in the world did a company like Polaroid, with a unique way to bring instant pictures to the world, miss the inflection point of digital imaging? Perhaps it was overconfidence, arrogance, or maybe even fear? Polaroid's stock fell from about $60.00 per share to $0.28 per share, illustrating beautifully the "die" phenomenon in the phrase "grow or die." Andrew Grove of Intel fame says, "There comes a point in time where you must change dramatically to reach new heights. Miss those points, and you will decline." A strategic organization or nation stays oriented externally and looks for these inflection points, plans for them, and adapts strategy based on them. A nonstrategic organization or nation simply fades into the sunset as it is replaced by a competitor who is oriented to the new reality, not the old.

What about IBM? IBM in Phase I was an idea and basic computer technology. IBM believed that the world of computing would be revolutionized and IBM would win that game with **superior computer hardware**. The idea was grown and developed and moved from Phase I to Phase II growth. IBM was the computer-hardware giant in the world even as new entrants to the market seemed to be focused on software. At the strategic inflection point for personal computers, it turned out that the new paradigm was one of software, not hardware, and that IBM had missed the inflection point. The company's hardware business began to fail and was so far behind the software competitors that it innovated itself into a service company. IBM not only survived but entered a new phase of substantial growth.

The purpose of this book is to generate dialogue about America, not Polaroid or IBM, but I hope the two examples we've covered give adequate context to look at our nation in terms of Phase I, II, and III growth. Let's look at what's happened to America since the 1950s in terms of the growth curve and examine how we will move forward and either grow or die. We are definitely at a strategic inflection point, as the math will prove.

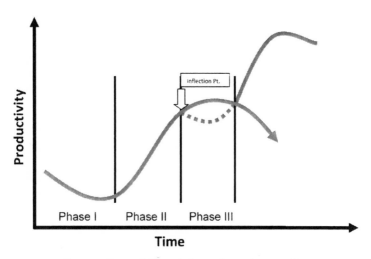

Source: Original Growth Curve from *Grow or Die* by Dr. George Land

Before picking up our growth curve analysis in the 1950s, it is worth looking at the fabric of our nation prior to the 1950s and, indeed, all the way back to our founding in 1776. At the core, America was a nation founded on the belief that individuals should be allowed maximum individual freedom, guided by a moral code that was solidly anchored in Judeo-Christian beliefs and **accountability** to God. Our founding fathers wrote and spoke often about the need for a moral compass, an anchor, in a nation where so much responsibility for proper behavior was going to be left to the individual. In fact, many of them worried out loud about what would happen to our great nation should that moral anchor and **accountability** to that higher power be diminished. American leaders throughout the short history of our nation used to speak publicly about the need for this same moral anchor—interesting foresight by some intellectual Americans you will most certainly recognize.

Samuel Adams, known as the father of the American Revolution wrote as the governor of Massachusetts in 1779:

> *A general dissolution of the principles and manners will more surely overthrow the liberties of America than the whole force of the common enemy. While the people are virtuous they cannot be subdued; but once they lose their virtue they will be ready to surrender their liberties to the first external or internal invader... If we would enjoy this gift of Heaven, let us become a virtuous people.*

Benjamin Franklin signed Pennsylvania's 1776 constitution, which stated:

> Each member of the legislature, before he takes his seat, shall make and subscribe the following declaration: "I do believe in one God, the Creator and Governour of the Universe, the Rewarder of the good and Punisher of the wicked, and I do acknowledge the Scriptures of the Old and

New Testament to be given by Divine Inspiration."

In 1798, President John Adams wrote, "Our Constitution was made for a moral and religious people. It is wholly inadequate to the government of any other."

In 1796, President George Washington said, "Of all the dispositions and habits which lead to political prosperity, Religion and Morality are indispensable supports. In vain would that man claim the tribute of Patriotism who should labor to subvert these great Pillars." He went on to say, "Reason and experience both forbid us to expect national morality can prevail in the exclusion of religious principle."

In 1950, President Harry S. Truman stated in his address to the Attorney General's Conference:

> The fundamental basis of this nation's laws was given to Moses on the Mount. The fundamental basis of our Bill of Rights comes from the teachings we get from Exodus and St. Matthew, from Isaiah and St. Paul. I don't think we emphasize that enough these days...If we don't have a proper fundamental moral background, we will finally end up with a totalitarian government which does not believe in rights for anybody except for the State.

In 1935, President Franklin Delano Roosevelt said this:

We cannot read the history of our rise and development as a nation, without reckoning with the place the Bible has occupied in shaping the advances of the Republic....Where we have been the truest and most consistent in obeying its precepts, we have attained the greatest measure of contentment and prosperity.

And finally, we have some Inaugural quotes from other presidents throughout America's history:

Franklin Roosevelt, 1945: "Almighty God has blessed our land."

Harry S. Truman, 1949: "We believe that all men are created equal because they are created in the image of God."

John F. Kennedy, 1961: "The rights of man come not from the generosity of the state but from the hand of God."

Richard Nixon, 1969: "As all are born equal in dignity before God, all are born equal in dignity before man."

Ronald Reagan, 1981: "With God's help, we can and will resolve the problems which now confront us. And after all, why shouldn't we believe that? We are Americans."

Before leaving this area, let me write down some rules for society and get your perspective. Does anything here seem like it would be contrary to good order in American society?

1. Don't steal from anyone.

2. Don't crave your neighbor's house.

3. Don't crave your neighbor's spouse.

4. Don't cheat on your spouse.

5. Don't kill anyone.

6. Honor your mom and your dad.

7. Don't lie about anyone.

8. Take one day off a week.

If we did all of those things, how would we be behaving as a society? Do we need a government to hold us accountable for these behaviors? If we simply hold ourselves accountable to these eight behaviors, would most of society's ills be quickly addressed? I'm sure many of you recognize that there are a couple of rules missing from this list of 10, but I've done that intentionally.

I purposely left the first two of the Ten Commandments out because I wanted this to at first be a test of basic societal **accountability** without injecting accountability to God. Our forefathers knew of the perils we could face in our society and seemed to know that either God or something else would be where Americans looked in time of peril. The Ten Commandments are the rules that our forefathers had in mind when they created our society based on individual freedom, and they were wary of a time when we might drift from that compass. Until the late 1950s and into the 1960s, *this reliance on and accountability to God formed the core of our nation's resilience.* Since then, many things have come together to push us to the strategic inflection point we face today; it was the move for some of America to "whatever feels individually good" in the '60s that started the ball rolling.

Our nation coming out of WWII had built the manufacturing powerhouse of the world and had developed great character while facing down a threat to our very existence. From the mid-1940s until the early 1970s, Americans were working hard and middle-class America was growing on that work ethic; our nation was enjoying Phase II growth. Then something happened; it was called consumer credit.

I remember my father saying in the 1970s that credit cards would be the death of America. I think he felt that way because he could see two potential devastating byproducts of access to easy credit. The first was a lack of **accountability** for the money that people actually spent. He knew people who had purchased things on credit that they couldn't afford and who were making minimum payments while their **accountability** for the total purchase price got more and more blurred over time. The second potential byproduct he saw was the lack of work ethic that followed easy credit. My father always worked a second job when we couldn't afford something that the family needed or wanted. I think he saw the ability to buy things without working for them to be a potentially fatal flaw in the backbone of America. If my father was alive today, I'm afraid he would feel he was seeing most of his initial misgivings about a credit-driven America playing out before his very eyes.

My question is this: Do we have the courage to correct our dependence on credit, and the willingness to reset our real standard of living to one that hasn't been propped up by $13 trillion of household debt? The current standard of living in America isn't real; it's a $13 trillion mirage. I believe we can and will reset our goals and, as Americans, make the right decisions based on what we can actually afford and hold ourselves **accountable** to those new numbers. Anything less than that will result in an America my father wouldn't recognize and one in which debt replaces choice and we have mortgaged the dreams of our children.

Since the mid-1960s, when America had only mortgage debt in terms of household debt, we have gone from a nation of people working two jobs to acquire something they wanted or needed to a nation of people who simply "put it on the card." Our current household debt is in the neighborhood of $12–13 trillion. Stated in mathematical terms, 1 million seconds is about 11.5 days, 1 billion seconds is about 32 years, while **1 trillion** seconds is equal to 32,000 years. Now multiply that by 13.

To get an idea of how big **1 trillion** is, look at this illustration from the Web comparing the build of an average human being against a stack of $100 currency bundles.

A bundle of $100 notes equivalent to $10,000 can easily fit in your pocket. One million dollars will fit inside a standard shopping bag, whereas a billion dollars would occupy a small room of your house.

Thus, 1 trillion (1,000,000,000,000) is 1000 times bigger than 1 billion and would therefore take up an entire football field—the man is still standing in the bottom left corner.

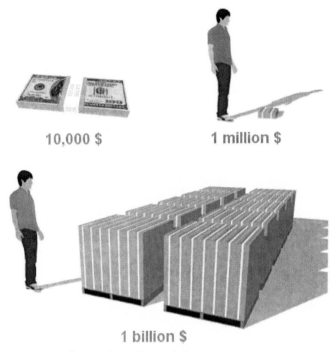

10,000 $

1 million $

1 billion $

Source: http://www.dailycognition.com

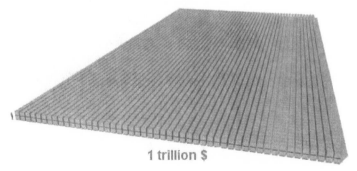

1 trillion $

Source: http://www.dailycognition.com

The nation's household debt would cover 13 football fields in pallets stacked approximately six feet tall with $100 bills. Our government debt is equivalent to our household debt, so add another $13 trillion of debt. We now have $26 trillion covering 26 football fields with those pallets. **America, we have a critical problem.**

How did it happen during what seemed like Phase II growth? Have we really been fooling ourselves all along? Let's look at all the effects that growing our household debt has had on our society, our businesses, our families, our politicians, and our psyche. Lastly, but maybe most importantly, what's the effect on our competitiveness as a nation, and what can we do about it?

If you go back to 1960 and look at our nation's household debt, you will see that it was almost zero. The only credit available to us as Americans was for very secure loans, primarily on homes with 20% or more as a down payment. As consumer credit came into being in the '70s, look at what happened to our trade deficits as a nation. I am not making the case for consumer credit being the only force at work here, but the trend line from the '70s is unmistakable. A trade balance is very simply the monetary difference between the value of the things we import and the value of the things we export. A trade deficit happens when we import more than we export.

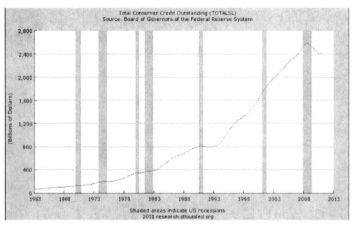

Source: Federal Reserve Bank of St. Louis,
http://research.stlouisfed.org

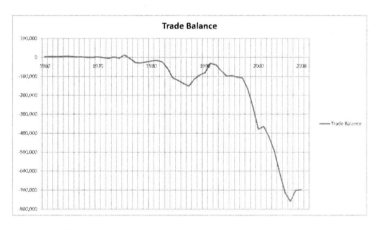

Source: Raw data from - www.census.gov/foreign-
trade/www/press.html

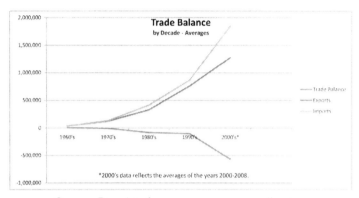

Source: Raw data from - www.census.gov/foreign-
trade/www/press.html

Period	Trade Balance	Exports	Imports
1960's	3,185	35,333	32,148
1970's	-8,214	122,584	130,798
1980's	-84,638	326,479	411,118
1990's	-105,912	755,608	861,519
2000's*	-571,282	1,272,565	1,843,847

*2000's data reflects the averages of the
years 2000-2008.

Source: Raw data from - www.census.gov/foreign-
trade/www/press.html.

Getting from almost zero debt to $13 trillion in debt hasn't been easy. It's actually taken entire industries to push easy credit upon us, and it's taken a lack of **accountability** by all of us to spend more than we can afford. The real challenge for us now is to determine how to starve the beast, because in terms of both our own households and our government, no one seems to be able to say no. **Our nation is at a strategic inflection point where failure is a real possibility if we don't begin to reorient ourselves to the new rules we now find ourselves in.**

The mortgage crisis shined a spotlight on how bonds are created and sold on Wall Street. What it failed to do is shine a similar spotlight on the bonds that are created, bought, sold, and bet against in the securities market with the rest of consumer debt. I am a former fighter pilot, not a Wall Street expert, but as I said earlier, one of the things we learned early in warfare preparation was to look at the big picture first. It is a known fact that our consumer debt is rolled into bonds, and a lot of people on Wall Street make money on those bonds, whether we pay our bills or not. The credit beast is big and well funded and completely linked to the politicians of both parties. It cannot be legislated away; we move too slowly in our democracy (sometimes a very good thing) to tactically outmaneuver Wall Street. We can do a better job at legislation that will protect consumer banking from investment banking, but ultimately, **we as consumers are going to have to starve the beast and hold ourselves and our elected officials** *accountable* **to that same standard.**

The number of jobs that have been created in the financial sector, housing sector, insurance industry, medical industry, and others as a result of our addiction to debt is staggering. We've seen the impact on some of these industries since 2008; there will be many more losers in the business world as we remove ourselves from our addiction to credit. That means jobs will be lost as industries whose only means of survival is cheap credit falter. **The truth is, we have to go through a real tough period in America to slowly let the air out of our credit-driven, consumption-based economy, and it's going to be painful. Think about the future of the politician who decides to tell us the truth. Would we vote for such a politician? If not, we are part of the problem.**

Unfortunately, we seem to still be living in denial as we try to borrow and spend our way out of a crisis when the math clearly requires us to downsize our appetites for things we can't afford at both the household and federal levels. We must work our way back to a production-driven economy, not a consumption-driven economy. We can consume all we can afford without over-borrowing and nothing more. When I was an airman, I went to the credit union to buy my first car in 1980. I showed the loan officer my application. She knew my rank and said, "Airman Modleski, we'll loan you eight hundred and fifty dollars to buy a car." I selected a white Plymouth Satellite Sebring with plaid seats and a red vinyl top with a tear in it. It was not what you would call a chick magnet, and because I was 18 years old, that mattered! So what did I do? I got a part-time job so I could move up in auto style.

The next major impact as a result of our addiction to debt is the impact on our productivity. Watching my dad as I grew up taught me that when you really want something or, more importantly, need something, a second job (or increased production) was the first option. Credit has made that less and less attractive for us, and even if people are willing to work a second job, the artificial economy that we're living in with 26 trillion borrowed dollars makes it hard to get by. Prices are artificially high (so are many salaries), but because we can borrow to pay them, we haven't dealt with what that's done to us as a nation. Through our 40-year journey of building a credit-based economy, prices have continued to rise while exported production has continued to fall (see the trade deficit). Our politicians have continued to make it easier and easier to access credit, never worrying about the country as a whole; they've simply worried about their next election cycle. We as Americans have been consumed with what we can "get" from our current position and stopped working to grow our education and skills as the basis for increased rewards. One day, we woke up and a fully bene-fitted high school graduate was making the same amount of money on an assembly line as a master's-educated nurse making life-and-death decisions, and then we wondered why we weren't competitive in manufacturing from a global perspective. Advanced education and continuous skill development used to be the drivers of personal growth and material success in America; now material goods are simply acquired using more and more credit. Every time we make an interest payment, we've paid a fee to "have" instead of an "investment to grow." Today, the federal debt is costing $1 billion a day. How do you think consumer credit rates compare to the rates the govern-ment is paying? They are at least double and could be approaching triple, which means annually, we are paying between $500 billion and $1 trillion in household interest to the financial sector instead of investing it in our skills, education, and innovative ideas.

Access to easy credit has made the difficult decisions that American companies should have faced years ago easy to cover up as our debt continued to climb and we didn't have to say no to anything. Both political parties share the blame; saying, "No, we can't afford it," has become almost impossible for the **career politicians** because we've given them open accounts at our expense. We have not held them **accountable** and in many ways have enabled them by not paying attention to how much our "wants" cost, and we keep sending the same establishment politicians back to DC over and over again. It will never get easier than it is today to fix this addiction; we have to start soon...the earlier the better.

The most important impact of easy credit on our society has been the impact on our families. With both spouses working and borrowing to keep up, we are contributing to the ever-spiraling credit bubble; in essence, we are feeding the beast. Money is also the number one reason for divorce in the nation (and with a divorce rate near 60%, the impact of our credit addiction on our society is huge). Once a divorce takes place, finances don't get easier; they get harder, and so more fuel is put on the fire. The impact on our society has been great and will continue to increase unless we can tame the credit addiction we have grown in the past 40 years.

Businesses that have grown accustomed to easy credit have come to face a grim reality recently: their businesses are always at risk. Many small businesses made a habit of making payroll with credit, and when the recent financial meltdown took place, they found themselves having to shutter their businesses or significantly downsize just to survive. Making payroll with credit may make sense for some businesses, but a business running week to week with large debt and poor cash flow is a **modern American business** built during our current love affair with debt. It's not a smart way to run a business. In the end, debt limits our choices and decision-making capability and may ultimately limit our freedom from both personal and business perspectives. It most assuredly impacts our national security and our global competitiveness.

I am going to mention our national security briefly here in relation to China. Later, when we talk about our path forward and global competitiveness, we will once again take a look at China and other nondemocratic up-and-comers on the world stage. General Sun Tzu, who lived some 2500 years ago, was a famous Chinese general who is often referred to as the father of strategy. General Sun never lost in battle, and so he was asked by his boss, General Woo, to write down his approach to warfare. Sun Tzu wrote *The Art of War* to fulfill his boss's request. In *The Art of War*, Sun Tzu articulates clearly that fighting a nation of great strength should be resisted if possible because during the fight, the precious resources of the conquered land will be destroyed. He taught that it is far better to be victorious without a fight than it is to go through the war. In China, nearly everyone reads *The Art of War* not as a part of some management class in college but as part of a cultural approach to life, business, and conflict. If I were assessing the main weaknesses of the US in terms of our population, I would say patience is a well-defined weakness for us. Knowing that we are not patient and based on our appetite for easy credit, one could say we have become undisciplined; a long and gradual takeover of the US through lending us money would make great sense to Sun Tzu. When I suggested this in the national security forum at the Air Force War College, several folks in our group argued that China needed us as a trading partner. My response was simple: Have you ever been the "junior partner" in a partnership? Who made all the decisions? Because the US has a printing press (therefore the ability to devalue our currency), China will be wary of overextending itself in terms of lending us money, but make no mistake…our inability to contain our appetite for credit and spending is a national security threat, and China is simply the most visible threat.

Moving Forward as a Nation

The world is moving faster and faster in terms of global competition. Would you agree? The very nature of the strategic inflection point that moves a nation from Phase II growth to a dip in productivity and then a resurgence in growth in Phase III (as depicted in the growth curve on page 72) is a change to the paradigm we were operating in before the inflection point. I would argue that the inflection point for America has been masked for some time by our addiction to debt and credit (see again our trade deficit), but the financial meltdown, our high unemployment rate, and the exodus of middle-class jobs for cheaper labor markets (based on the skill required) is the new reality. Going back to "the way things were before" won't work any better for America than it would have worked for Polaroid once they missed the digital revolution in film. We must work within the new set of rules. Let's talk about the resource of time and how it's used relative to our global competitiveness.

Global Competition

Time is the one constant in the world. Each day has 24 hours or, if you prefer, 1440 minutes or 86,400 seconds.

We can all agree on those mathematical realities, and we can also agree that if everyone played by the same rules, time would be a level playing field, regardless of the competitive scenario.

The challenge with this premise is that when in competition, most strategic competitors are seeking a competitive advantage and don't want to play by the same set of rules. They seek to establish the rules by which the game is played. Their goal is to shape the competitive metrics so their strengths may be clearly positioned against a competitor's weakness.

Infamous US Air Force fighter pilot and strategist John Boyd (infamous because he was brilliant yet brashly opinionated and not aligned with Air Force thinking at the time) first realized that time was not a level playing field while flying and fighting in the USAF Fighter Weapons School. He realized that even against a superior competitive aircraft, he could *achieve victory by controlling the tempo of the decisions made* and, in effect, use that compression of time to confuse a competitor to the point that the competitor either gave up or made a very serious and fatal mistake. It was many years later that Boyd put what he learned about fighter aircraft into practical strategic language, but the message was the same. Every competitor, every nation, has a **decision cycle time,** and the crucial fact that's important is this: either your decision cycle is faster than your competitor's or you are reacting to a competitor who is controlling the situation with a faster decision cycle.

One of the easiest examples I can come up with in America to illustrate decision-cycle speed is the use of the no-huddle offense in football. In the no-huddle offense, the quarterback of the offense compresses time by not huddling, thereby controlling the tempo of the game and putting the defensive team in a reactionary mode. By consistently forcing the defense to react to the offensive moves, the offense gains the strategic advantage in terms of time (assuming they can tactically execute). The Indianapolis Colts have made a living for years by operating inside their competitor's decision cycles, and the 2010 Oregon Ducks played for an NCAA football national title by executing the same strategy.

John Boyd defined and characterized decision-cycle time with the term OODA loop (**O**bserve, **O**rient, **D**ecide, and **A**ct). The OODA loop has been written about by Robert Coram in a biography entitled *Boyd* and by Chet Richards in his book, *Certain to Win*.

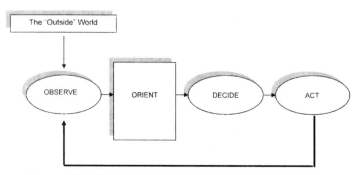

Source: Chet Richards, from John R. Boyd's The Essence of Winning and Losing, http://dnipogo.org/john-r-boyd/

I could continue to write on and on about Boyd's OODA loop, but the critical aspect of it for our purposes is this: As a democracy and—more accurately stated—as a large "bureaucracy," we are slow when compared to other, more autocratic, forms of government. This is a decided disadvantage in terms of global competition. Even scarier in terms of global competitiveness is that instead of shrinking the size of our government agencies, we have grown them larger, making our decision cycles even longer and inhibiting our ability to compete globally. This disadvantage in decision-cycle speed also gives an advantage to a smaller, more nimble competitor when working domestically.

Do you think a tactical piece of legislation by Congress aimed at Wall Street can be executed faster than Wall Street can find the next opportunity to exploit? The answer is probably no; therefore, tactical pieces of legislation will simply add bureaucracy instead of truly solving our problems. Strategic legislation requires courage and a distancing of politicians from the influence of Wall Street money. (Barack Obama took $900,000 from Goldman Sachs in his 2008 campaign; hedge funds on Wall Street contributed $10,000,000 to Republican campaigns in 2010. Does anyone in their right mind think that doesn't buy influence?) Strategic legislation would be focused on separating the investment banks from commercial banks like they used to be prior to the repeal of the Glass–Steagall Act in 1999. This repeal effectively removed the separation that had existed between Wall Street investment banks and depository banks. The net result for us average Americans is that our exposure to Wall Street risk-taking increased dramatically. We should demand that the firewall be put back in place. Before the barrier was removed, the investment banks were allowed to fail if they were poor businesses. Once they were connected to the commercial lenders, however, they had US-backed security to take massive gambles, and they lined politicians' pockets with campaign cash to keep that cozy relationship in place. Just look at the contributions over time by Wall Street firms to influential politicians. It's easy to see why we have the mess we have, but we can fix it. The sound bites from both parties rail against Wall Street excess; however, the action taken by our politicians solidifies the money machine for their campaigns with our taxpayer-guaranteed dollars backing risky investment practices. The engine of growth in the financial sector comes right back to the easy availability of consumer credit, and we must limit our appetite for that credit if we want to put America back on solid ground. The 536 people running the country—435 in the House, 100 in the Senate, and the president—have proven too career-minded, too slow, too corrupt, or all three to meaningfully guide our nation, so it is up to us to hold them accountable and simultaneously starve the beast, our credit addiction.

The recession and its unemployment, our massive debt (both household- and government-owned), and the expectations of a society that has "grown up" during this spending spree have all contributed to our current dilemma. We have reached our strategic inflection point and have begun a slow decline in Phase III. **We have no inherent right to continue as a great nation**. We are going to have to work for it! We can recover and "grow" to become the nation all of us want for our children, but the rules have changed and we must adapt to the new realities. Going back to the way things used to be is not an option once the rules change, just ask Polaroid. Those voices that yearn for what we tried in the 1930s must understand that the math has changed. We're paying interest on $26 trillion and have inflated our standard of living based on that borrowing. The combined interest payment on household debt and government debt is nearly $1 trillion per year. Our adjustments will not be easy as we shrink our massive addiction to credit and correct our standard of living. As a result, many industries will contract, and job losses will occur. That's the bad news. The good news is, once we decide what our new "competitive advantage" is as a nation, it will be much easier to fuel the future with tactical activity that links to that strategy. Many of us may make a little less money doing what we do as we are weaned from our addiction to credit and consumption. Our standard of living in America is now based on a total of $26 trillion of debt. **As we stop buying things we can't afford, it will appear as if our standard of living is declining, but in reality, we will simply be resetting it to a sustainable standard that we can afford.** The good news is, once we are no longer looking at the $13 trillion mirage called household debt, we can get back to earning real raises in a real, productive economy.

Our National Revival

Our nation is at a critical point in its short history, a strategic inflection point. We are looking at a future clouded in uncertainty, shrouded in debt, and polarized more politically than most of us have seen in our lifetimes. It is at these times that we need to remember why our great nation was formed, the principles upon which she was built, and the fact that although it is not perfect in any sense, there is no place better on earth to pursue one's dream.

If you believe that the speed of competitive decision making is simply going to increase as the world becomes more connected, you likely agree that the first obvious challenge for our nation is to shrink government to the point that it can operate efficiently and inside many competitor's OODA loops. As I mentioned earlier, a democracy by its nature is going to make decisions more slowly than an autocratic counterpart is, so where will our competitive advantage come from? The place it has always come from; **the American people.**

Once we have weaned ourselves from the addiction to credit, we will see living within our means as the only method to drive meaningful innovation in small businesses. Paying interest first and investing in new ideas second simply starves resources from the new ideas. It would be wonderful if we could borrow and spend our way back to being a production-based economy instead of a consumption-based economy, but the reality is, every time we borrow money, we give away choices and freedom to whoever made us that loan. The competitive spirit that lives in the fabric of America is ultimately what will save our nation, but only if we are willing to get off the credit addiction **and get back to an accountable approach to American life.**

How We Move Forward

Big Dreams

The power of a big dream has always been the beauty in America. We have fought for our freedoms more times than we care to count, and we have even fought amongst ourselves when it was clear that individual freedom for all really meant ALL. America has never been about the guaranteed result; rather, it has always been about guaranteeing the opportunity. With the power of big dreams, America's potential can be realized, and having the freedom to pursue those dreams remains America's greatest gift. We are not perfect; no society will ever be perfect, but having lived around the world, I know there is no place like America to pursue one's dream.

Accountability and Competitive Spirit

One of the keys to our future success as a nation needs to be flexibility in our skill sets and a renewed focus and appreciation for the benefits of continuing education. We need to look at the world as a world-class athlete looks at his or her competitors: with admiration for their ability and a competitive spirit that makes winning our obsession. Our massive addiction to credit has devalued the difference that we see between what increased education can "buy" compared with the limits that come with a lack of education. Notice I didn't say a "college education" (talk about a credit-driven inflation of prices, just ask your friends how many of them took a home equity line of credit to pay for their children's college); I simply said education. America has always been a nation that rewards increased education, improved skills and strong work ethics. Easy credit dilutes the "easy-to-see" advantages that come with higher and more diverse education and improved skills because it makes acquiring material goods easy without doing all the hard work.

Most of the jobs our kids will fill (my boys are ten and six in 2011) aren't even on the drawing board yet as the competitive global landscape develops; therefore, we must help our children and young adults find their core talents, develop those talents, and also develop multiple skills using those talents. Multiple skills will permit a flexible workforce, and linking those skills to core talents will yield a high-performance workforce as our children will learn to work in areas that are natural fits for their strengths instead of just places to make a buck. We must also help our children learn to be more disciplined with their credit than my generation has been—much more disciplined! Small businesses will provide most of the new jobs in America; we must be flexible in the skills we bring, and we must reward small-business owners who are willing to risk their hard-earned capital to bring their businesses to life and put people to work. The competitive spirit in America is alive and well. Exercising **accountability** in our use of credit and tapping into a flexible, skilled, and competitive workforce will yield growth in the new reality that is global competition.

Perseverance

America has always been a country that has persevered. From the early settlers fighting the American wilderness to the many Americans today reaching for and accomplishing their dreams, perseverance has always been a core competence of true Americans. Our national resolve is going to be tested in ways that most of us haven't seen in our lifetimes. We will have to endure challenges in terms of employment opportunities as many of the jobs created by the $26 trillion mirage disappear. We will have family challenges as those we know and love struggle as our consumption- and credit-driven economy is reoriented to one of production. But I have complete faith in our nation and in our people. In the end, we will persevere and move our nation into a new, more nimble era of production and growth through hard work and perseverance.

Family and Faith

Our elected officials are not telling us the complete truth. America is in for a very rough stretch as we draw the excesses out of our standard of living and reorient our economy to one of production and not consumption. The reliance on faith and family has long been a foundational element in American society. We have moved further and further away from being comfortable talking about faith, family, and **accountability** in the public square. For example, we have moved the **accountability** for taking care of our elderly parents to a "benefit" that should be covered through insurance policies. We can't come close to affording to have someone else pay for taking care of all of our aging family members into the future. As a nation, the math doesn't add up; in fact, it doesn't come close. I would ask this simple question: Do you think we are better off now as a society as we have drifted further from **accountability** to our original national moral compass than we were in the middle part of our Phase II growth? We are going to have to strengthen our family commitments to one another, strengthen our trust in God, and help one another through this decline in our national production. Here in the beginning of Phase III, we are experiencing a dip in performance. Growth will follow if we have the courage to tell the truth and reorient ourselves to the new paradigm, which is global competition. Poorer nations and some of the poorest elements of our nation, by necessity, do a good job of taking care of one another because they have no other options. We should all prepare to help one another with faith and family, as the years ahead are going to be tough. We will emerge stronger as a result!

The Legend of Big Daddy

I was 46 years old when I went to Disney World for the first time, and I must say it was an impressive place. The engineering, the attention to detail, the cleanliness—it was, well, magical. It was also very expensive to take a family of four, but we had saved the money and took our two boys, then ages seven and four, to see Mickey and his friends. We had fun and ran around the park, exhausted ourselves over several days, and returned home "Mickey'd out." The only time Disney World has come up in our house since we visited the Magic Kingdom was when one of us parents brought it up. The kids have essentially put it in their memory banks, and my guess is it resides next to cool movies they have seen and cool Legos they have built. Let's fast-forward to the summer of 2010.

It was a spring day, and it had rained hard. I had promised the boys that we could go fishing together in the local retention pond. The pond had some big fish in it, but the typical action was a bite from a four-inch sunfish every cast and occasionally some luck reeling one in. On this day, I was setting the hook for my younger boy, Jacob, when, all of a sudden, his little sunfish pole bent straight over, and the line went out tight and snapped, the fish was gone! I said to Jacob, "That was a big fish, buddy. I think it was big daddy." The legend of Big Daddy was born, and from that day on, as we drove past the pond, the discussion would ensue about what kind of fish Big Daddy was and how big he must be. We fished many more times over the spring, hoping to catch Big Daddy, and sure enough, it finally happened.

Both my son and I had lines in the water, and I had a small nibble that seemed like every other sunfish, until I set the hook. I yelled over to Jacob to get the net, and when he looked at the pole, he screamed, "It's Big Daddy!" Jacob moved up and down the shoreline as he positioned the net to bring Big Daddy ashore. After about 10 minutes and some help from a passerby, we netted Big Daddy, a huge catfish that we had managed to hook very gingerly in the lip. Another passerby took the pictures below as Jacob got an up-close view of Big Daddy. Here's the best part: For the better part of one month straight, Jacob shared the legend of Big Daddy with anyone who would listen. He related the history, the story, and all the details he could remember or embellish! It was absolutely awesome! The real lesson for me as an American dad was the time I've spent at the pond's edge with my sons, a few worms, and Big Daddy were worth more in terms of memories, for all of us, than a trip to Disney World that cost several thousand dollars!

Summary

The United States of America is at a strategic inflection point, a time in our history when we must reorient ourselves to our competitive environment in order to grow, or we will die. The mathematical realities facing our nation are unprecedented. Our addiction to credit-driven consumption has bartered our freedom; our political system and the politicians in it seem unable or unwilling to address the true nature of the problem because that means pain for all of us. Our nation has begun the Phase III decline that happens when the strategic inflection point occurs, but that does not mean the end of our nation unless we choose to ignore the peril. **Don't look for someone else to fix it, America! We hold the keys to our future, not someone else. Here is a starting point and our call to action:**

1. Live within our means; reduce our credit addiction and our household debt. We must set household objectives that are SMART to steadily buy freedom by reducing interest payments to others. We must hold ourselves **accountable.**

2. There are no shortcuts to success in America. Happiness is achieved when we live within our means, build meaningful relationships with family and friends, and join forces to accomplish something bigger than ourselves, and by working hard and improving ourselves each day. The rise in the use of consumer credit, the dot-com bust, and now the housing crisis have all shined a light on the fact that if it looks too good to be true, it is. Dream big, and then outwork everyone else with the same dream—that's the Amer-

ican way. Let's hold ourselves **accountable** and be dream enablers for someone else, especially our children.

3. We must demand a balanced federal budget, which will require a sizeable reduction in the federal government but will yield increased competitiveness in terms of faster decision cycles by moving more decisions into the states or removing government involvement completely. Hold congressmen, senators, the president and other elected officials **accountable.**

4. We must elect leaders who will tell us the truth. Don't believe anyone who says we can work our way out of our financial dilemma without any pain. It is untrue, and whoever says it can be painless cannot be trusted to make hard choices. Elect officials who will tell us the truth, and hold them **accountable.**

5. We must demand that companies too big to fail be given a 12–18 month period to restructure themselves into businesses that can fail for poor business practices. Hold congressmen, senators, the president and other elected officials **accountable.**

6. We must find and support courageous leaders who want to serve America, not build DC-based careers in politics (through self-limited terms, for example). We must take more interest in and be more **accountable** for who we send to represent us. We deserve the government we continue to elect.

7.   We must demand a legislative firewall between investment banks and commercial, FDIC-insured lenders. Hold congressmen, senators, the president and other elected officials **accountable** to do this, and don't accept excuses.

8.   We must reestablish our family priorities for time together instead of credit-driven adventures (remember Big Daddy). Hold ourselves **accountable** for quality time to grow our families.

9.   If you are a believer in God, give the gift of strong faith in God to your children and be **accountable** for the example you set; it will help them immensely.

10.   Work with our children to identify their core strengths and talents, and focus on **developing** multiple skills in them through diverse education and skill-building experiences. We, not the local school, are **accountable** for our children's education. Foreign nations are kicking our butts in this department!

11.   Our politicians must articulate **SMART objectives** in terms of reducing our debt addiction. A good example of such an objective would be "reduce federal spending by 7% per year for the next five years." SMART objectives are essential before we can establish a strategy, so we must hold our politicians **accountable** to set SMART objectives.

12. Make value-based decisions on college and vocational-skill development and focus on diversified skills. Ask ourselves, how much difference is there in terms of the value of education our kids are getting for what we're paying? Most colleges are way over-priced for the value received because we have all been trained to get home equity lines of credit, or another type of credit, to feed the credit beast and over-pay for college (see chart below). Teenage kids don't have the wisdom to make this decision; we have to be the ones **accountable** to set the parameters based on the best value we can afford.

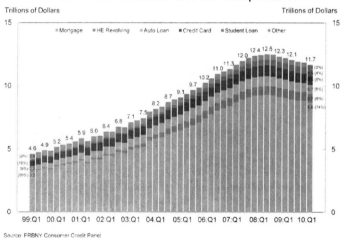

Total Debt Balance and its Composition

Source: Federal Reserve Bank of New York, Quarterly Report on Household Debt and Credit, August 2010.
http://www.newyorkfed.org/research/national_economy/householdcredit/DistrictReport_Q22010.pdf, page 3

13. Have trust in the goodness of America. We are a wonderful nation of people with a foundation in faith and a competitive spirit that has served us well for our entire existence. We will be stronger for the challenges that lie ahead, and we must be **accountable** for the changes we wish to see!

Conclusion

The American Dream is alive and well in the hearts of nearly every person I know. We control our destiny. A strong faith in God and a helping hand to our neighbors will be required for us to grow out of our current dilemma, and most importantly, **we must be accountable to live within our means and hold our elected officials to that same standard.** If we won't do those two things and pay the price for the $26 trillion in excesses that we have accumulated, then most assuredly, we won't be leaving the American Dream to our children; instead, they'll be reading about it in very different-sounding history books than the ones we've read. I believe we can make the necessary changes, do you? If so, join me as I seek to engage 1% of America in the "American Dream" dialogue. Once we have 1% of America connected in our efforts, we can meaningfully change the trajectory of our great nation. Let's be **accountable** and make it happen!

About the Author
Matthew M. Modleski

Matt was born in East Chatham, New York. There he learned the values of family, faith, perseverance and big dreams. Matt enlisted in the Air Force at age seventeen, and served as jet engine mechanic and air traffic controller, before earning his commission in 1987. He is a recipient of the Distinguished Flying Cross and has logged over 120 hours of combat time. After overcoming numerous obstacles and challenges, he accomplished his American Dream and became a pilot for the Thunderbirds!

Since retiring from the Air Force, Matt has worked in the healthcare marketplace as a corporate executive, and as an equity business partner in a strategy and leadership consulting firm, Stovall Grainger Modleski Inc. Matt developed a leadership course called Active Leadership® and has spoken extensively on the subject.

Matt resides in Carmel, IN with his wife Dianne and their two sons, Keaton and Jacob.

CPSIA information can be obtained at www.ICGtesting.com
Printed in the USA
LVOW06s1917211213

366354LV00001B/1/P